Fierce, Fabulous & Feminine

Always Authentic Never Jeopardizing Individuality

I0392527

All Artwork by

Phyllis Anne Taylor

"Pannet"

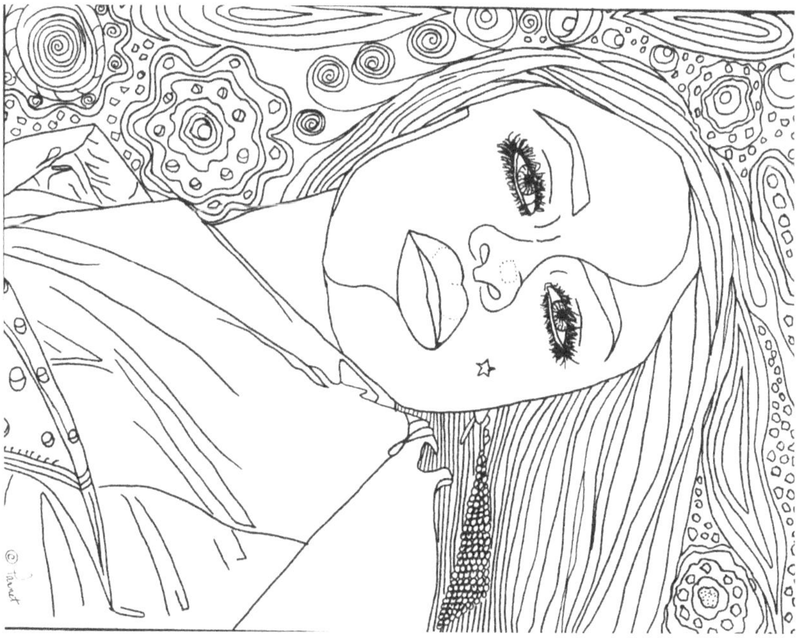

ISBN: 13:9781537320687

ISBN: 10:1537320688

This book is dedicated to all the Women and Mighty Girls' I know and love.

This coloring book of *Fierce* & *Fabulously Feminine Women* was created when I found that many other adult coloring books were more stressful, to me, than they were relaxing! Many of the adult coloring books are so filled with minute details they give the eye no place to rest causing distress or confusion to many. Listening to others, in book stores and places where adult coloring books are sold, who expressed my same concerns convinced me to proceed.

The *Fierce & Fabulously Feminine Women* in this coloring book are all a part of my life, real and imagined! This adult coloring book will appeal to both lovers of portraits and to those who love intricate detail and creativeness.

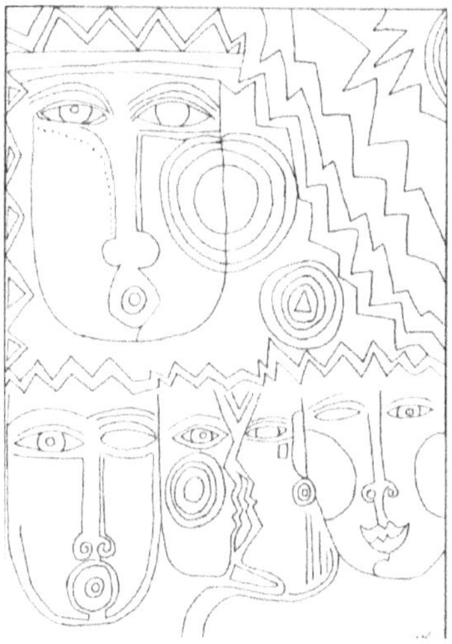

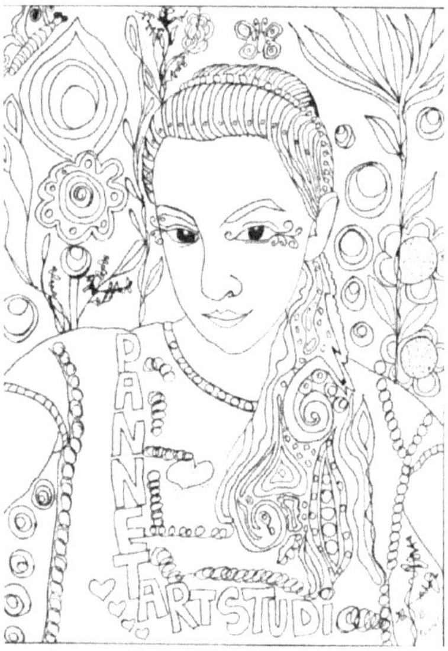

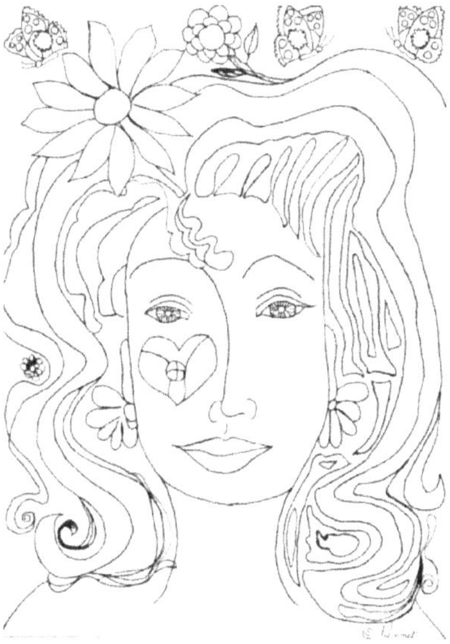

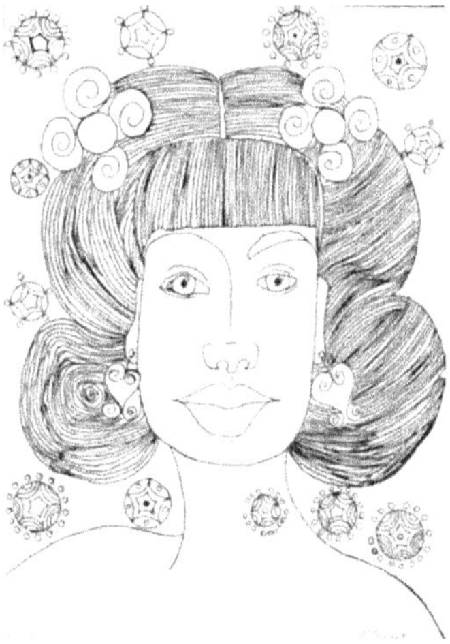

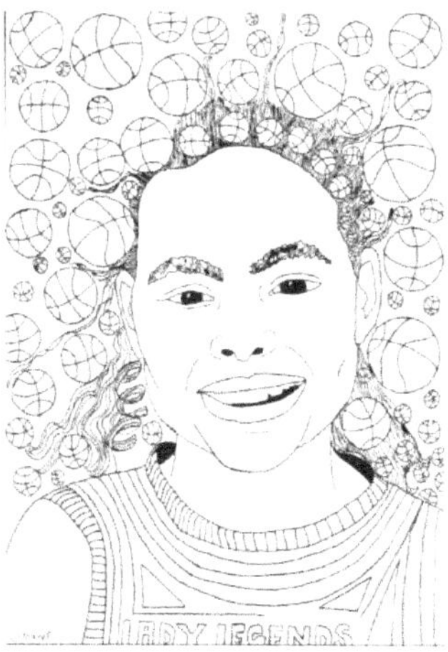

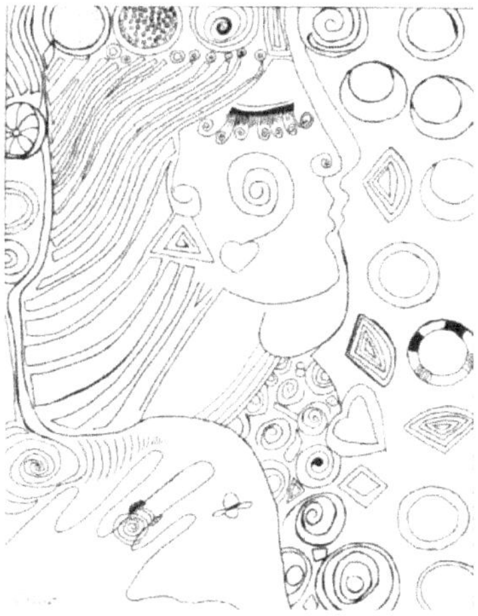

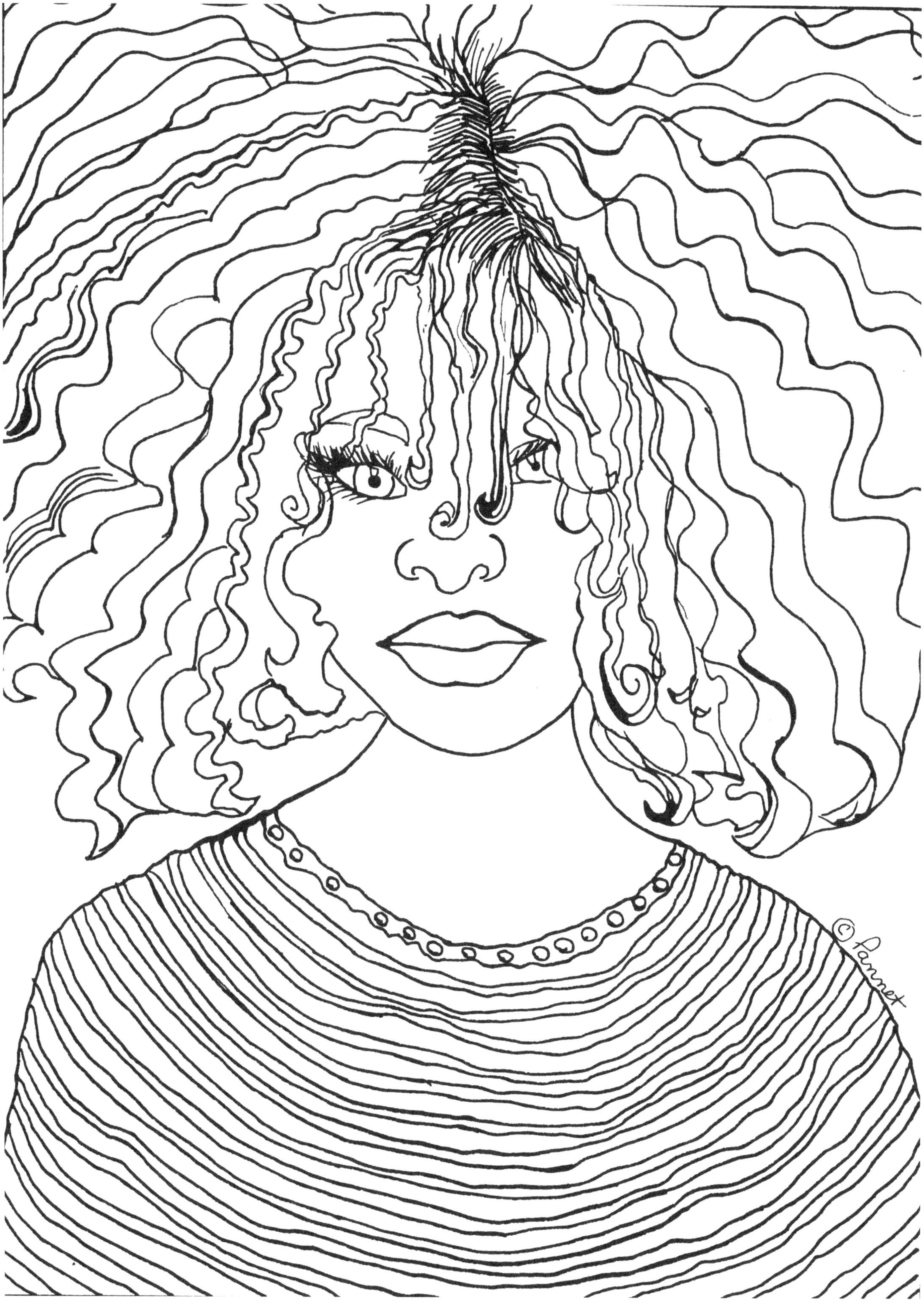
© Pannet

January

Sunday	Monday	Tuesday	Wednesday	Thursday	Friday	Saturday

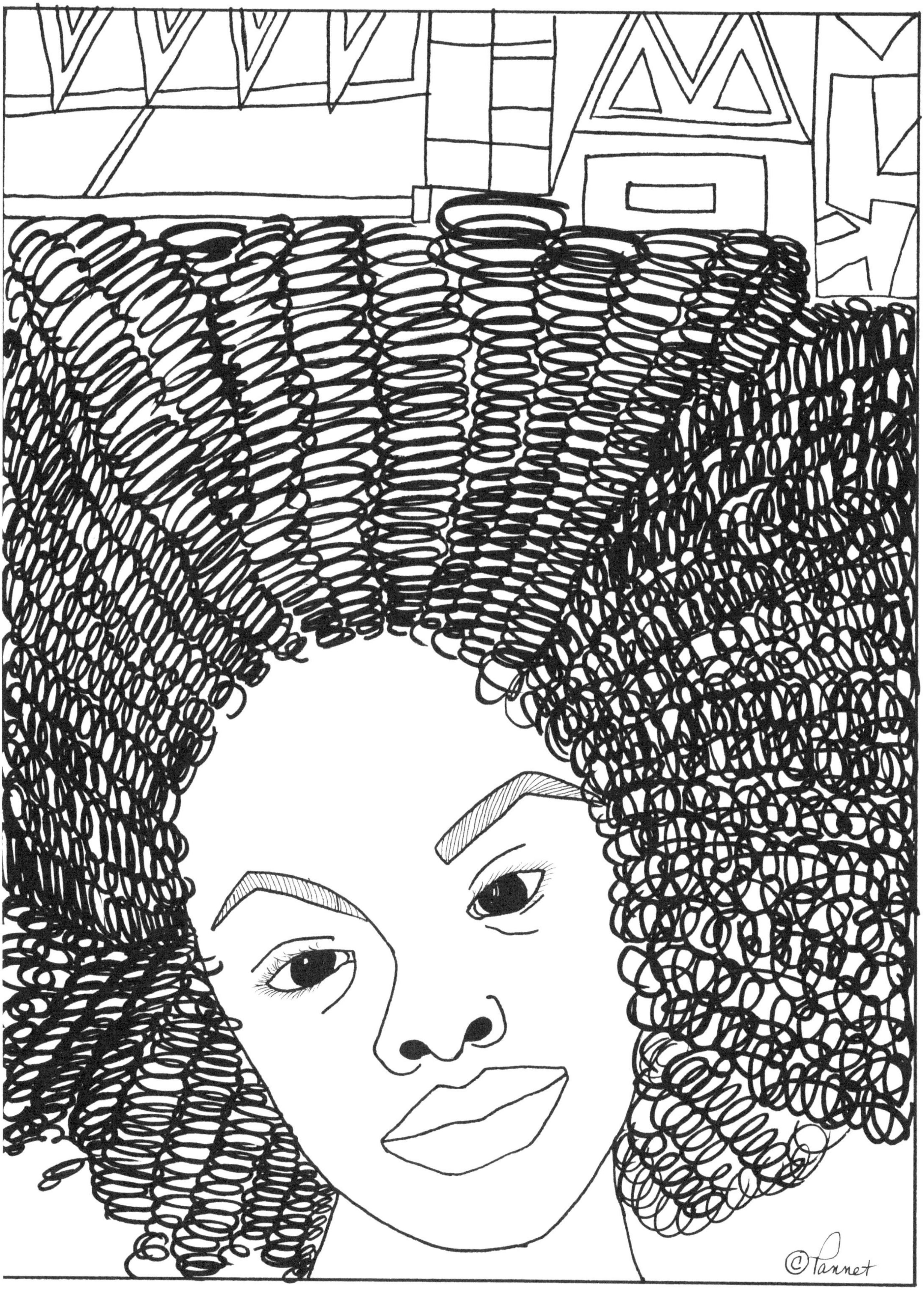
©Pannet

February

Sunday	Monday	Tuesday	Wednesday	Thursday	Friday	Saturday

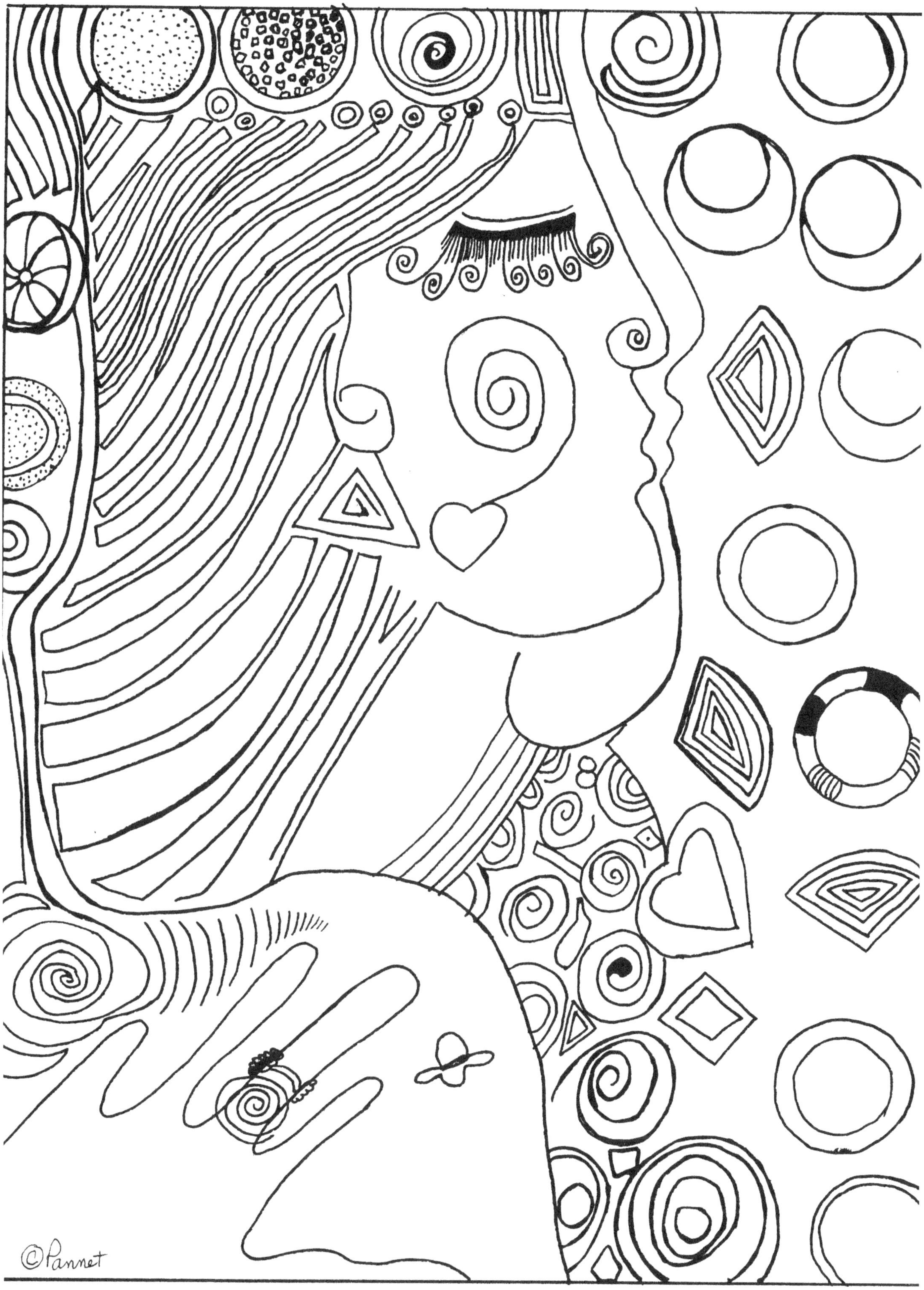

©Pannet

March

Sunday	Monday	Tuesday	Wednesday	Thursday	Friday	Saturday

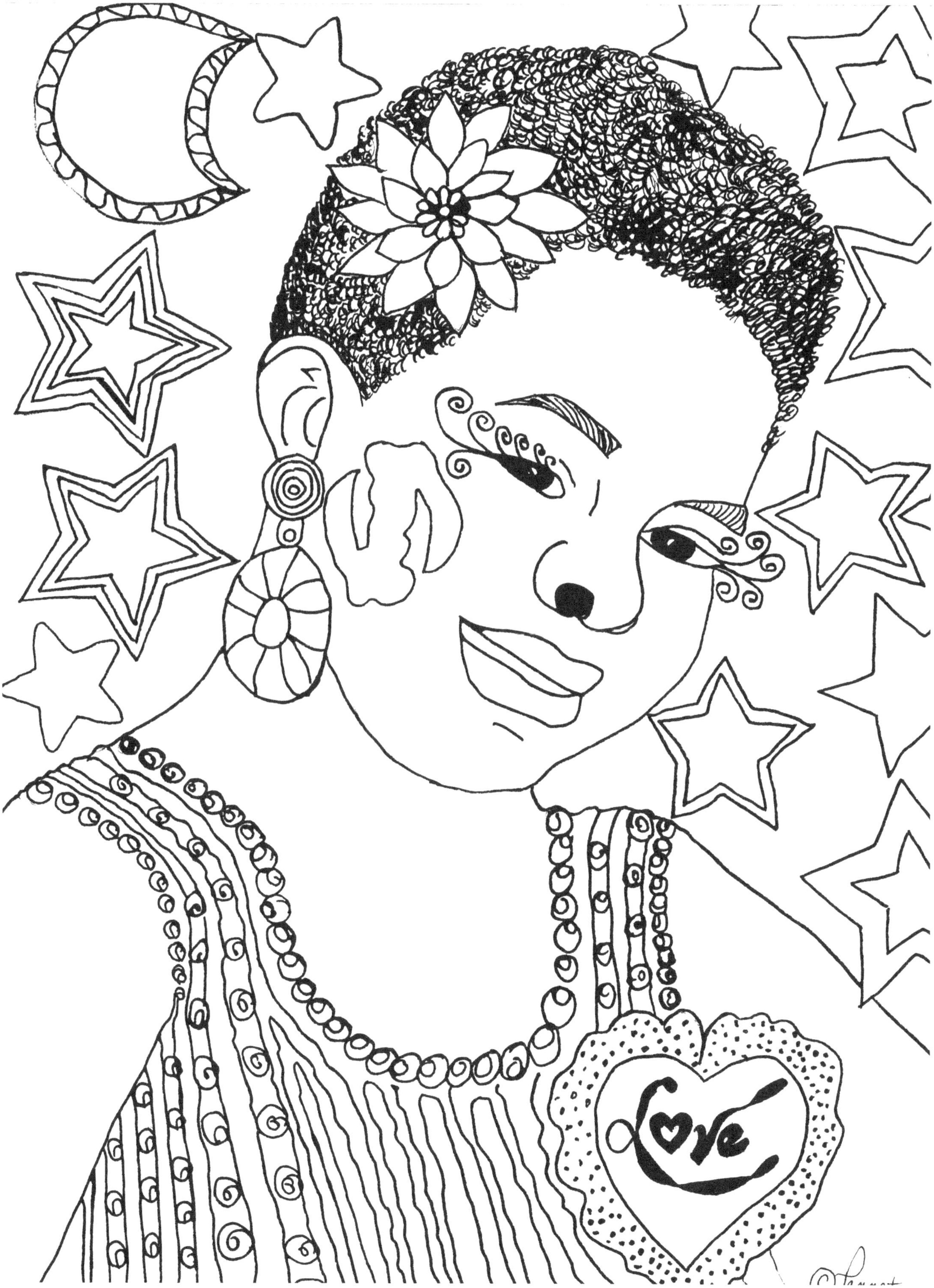
Love

April

Sunday	Monday	Tuesday	Wednesday	Thursday	Friday	Saturday

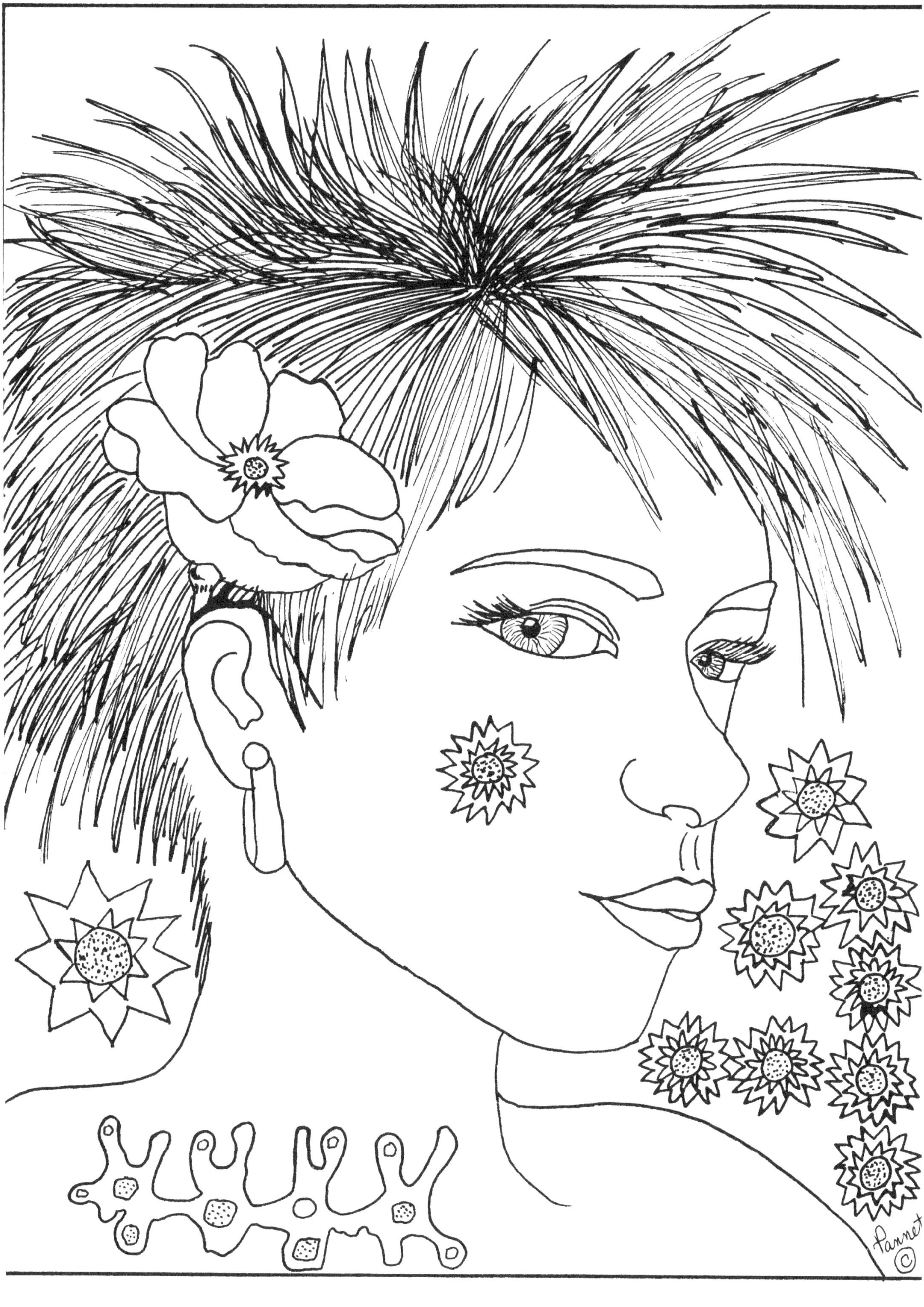
Pannet
©

May

Sunday	Monday	Tuesday	Wednesday	Thursday	Friday	Saturday

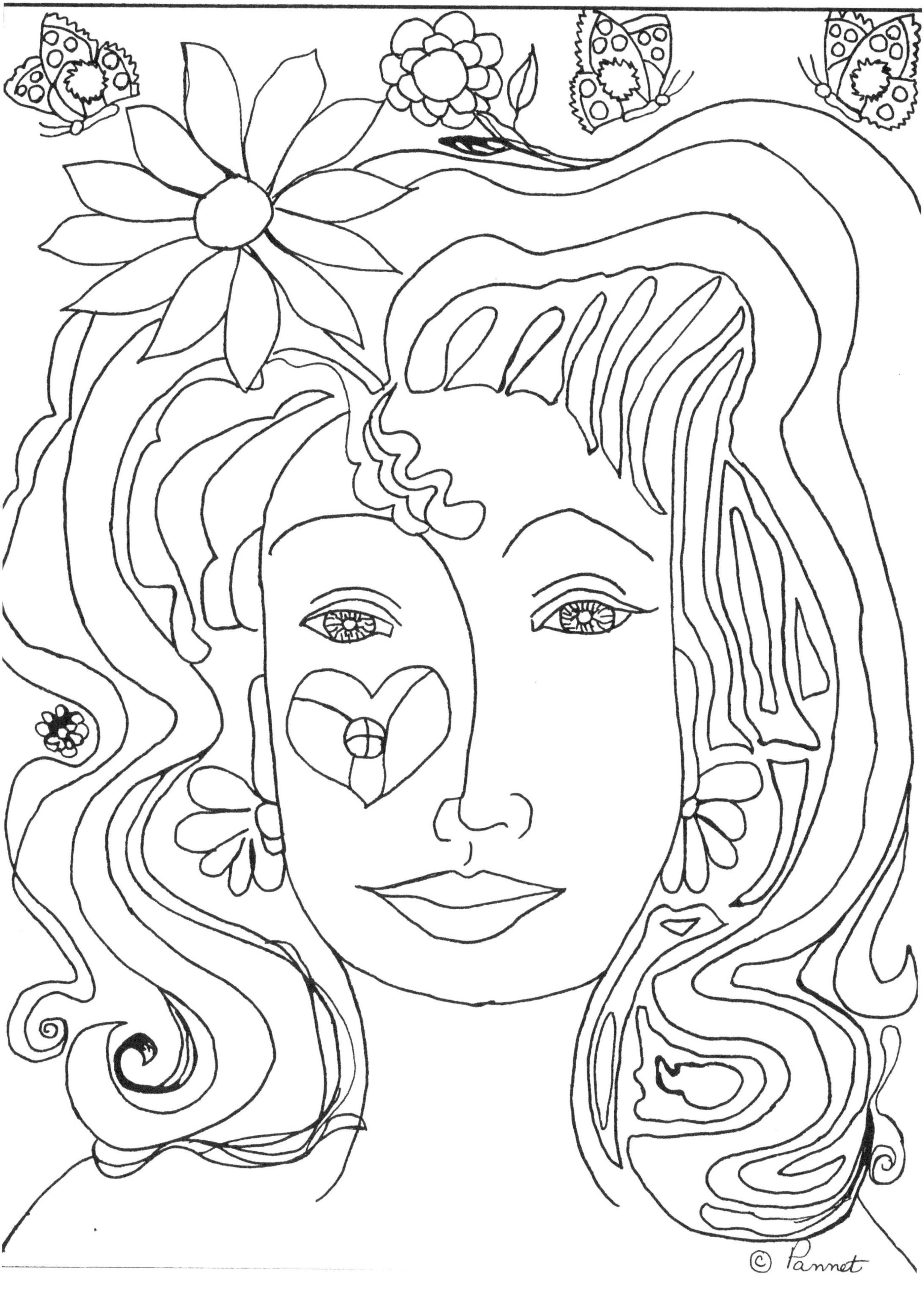

June

Sunday Monday Tuesday Wednesday Thursday Friday Saturday

Sunday	Monday	Tuesday	Wednesday	Thursday	Friday	Saturday

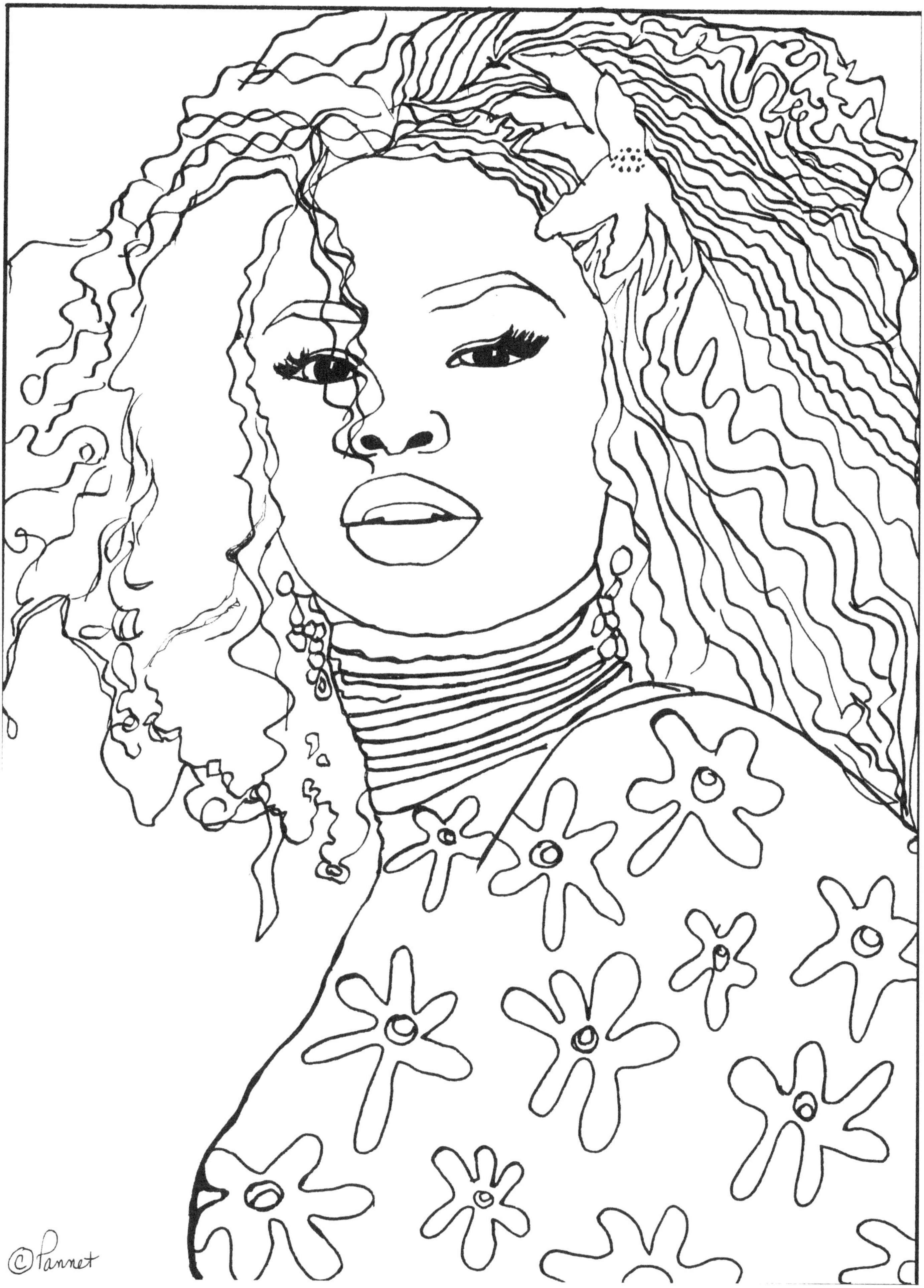

July

Sunday	Monday	Tuesday	Wednesday	Thursday	Friday	Saturday

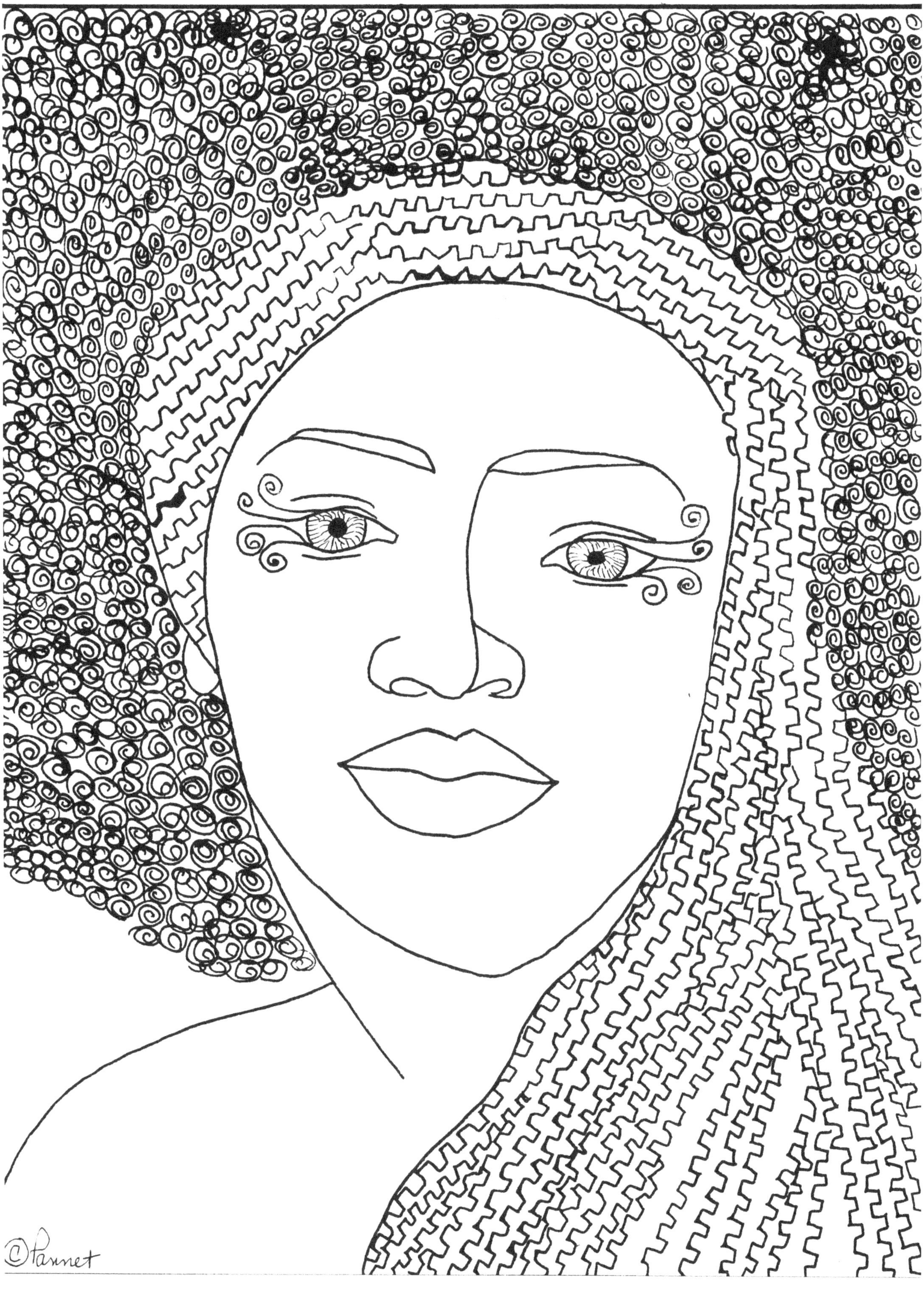
©Pannet

August

Sunday	Monday	Tuesday	Wednesday	Thursday	Friday	Saturday

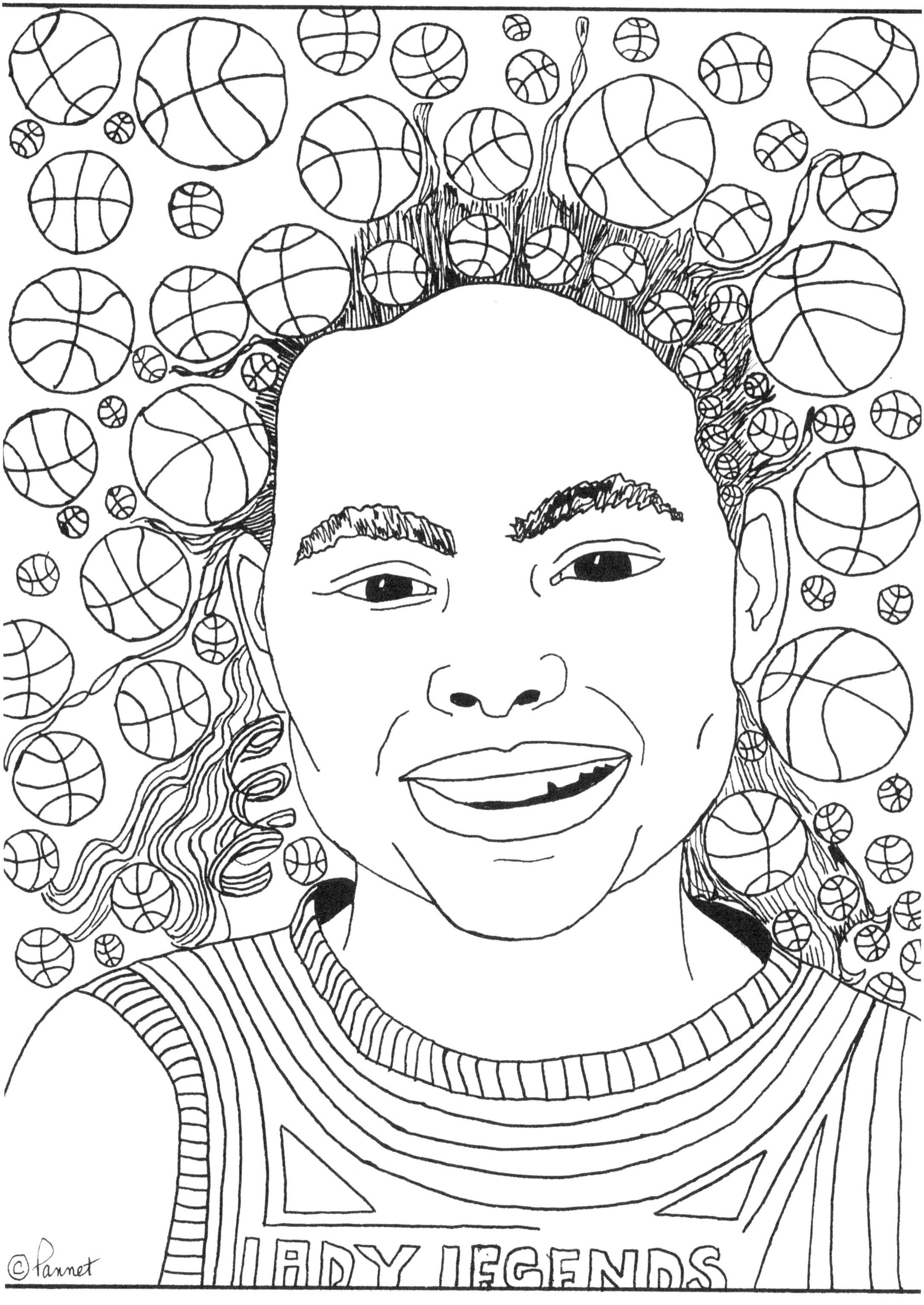
LADY LEGENDS
©Pannet

September

Sunday	Monday	Tuesday	Wednesday	Thursday	Friday	Saturday

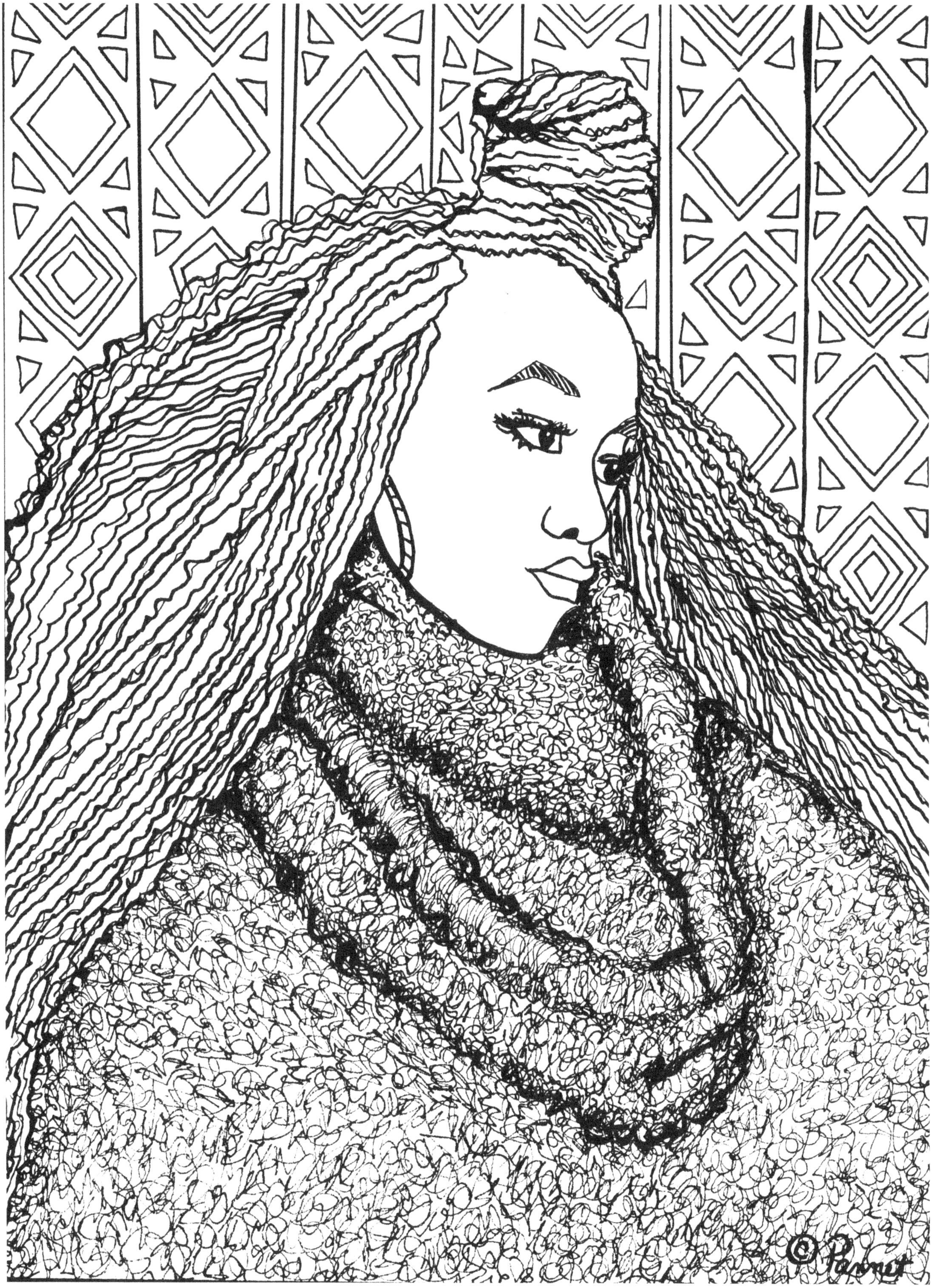
© Parmer

October

Sunday	Monday	Tuesday	Wednesday	Thursday	Friday	Saturday

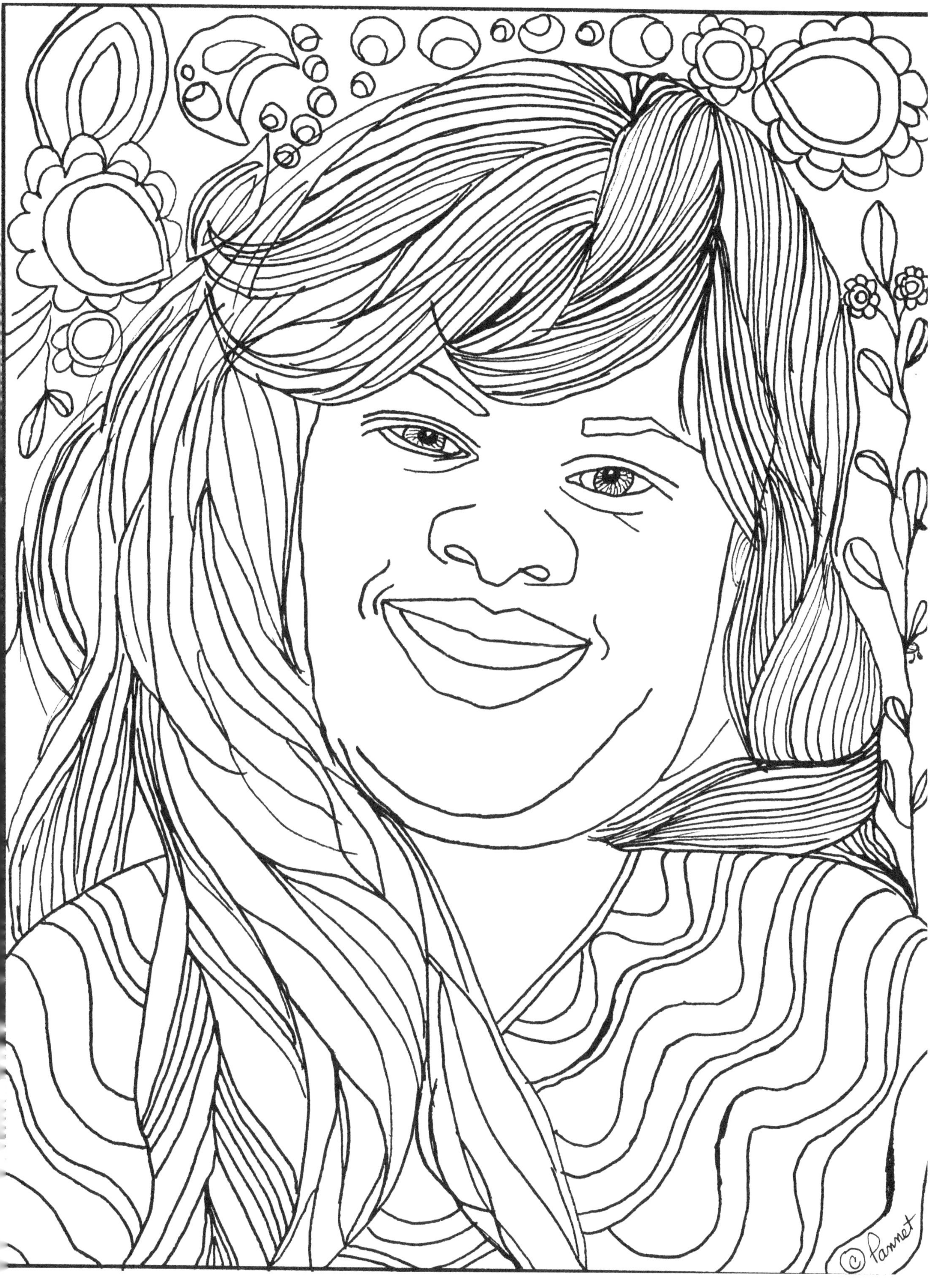
© Pannet

November

Sunday	Monday	Tuesday	Wednesday	Thursday	Friday	Saturday

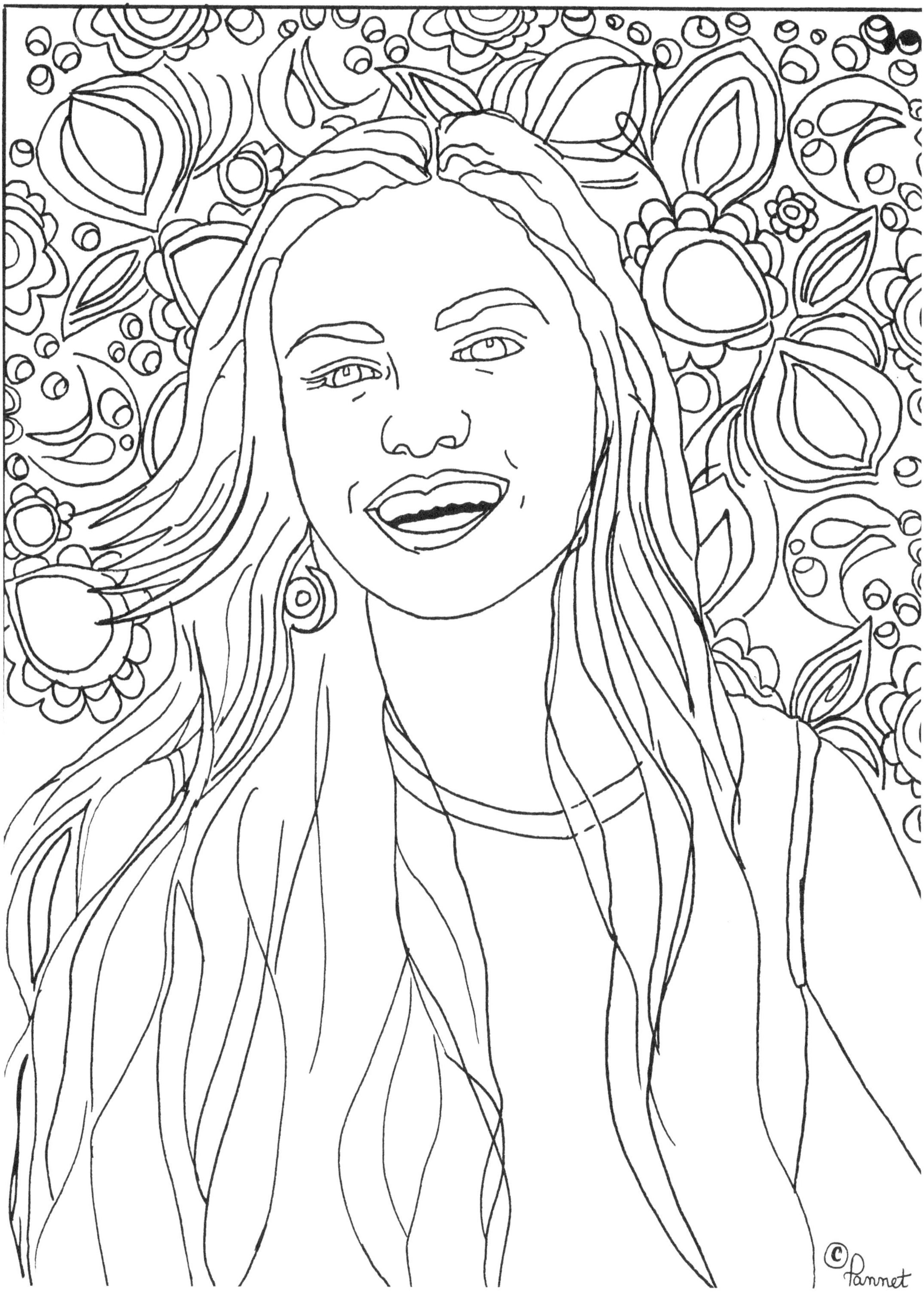
© Pannet

December

Sunday	Monday	Tuesday	Wednesday	Thursday	Friday	Saturday

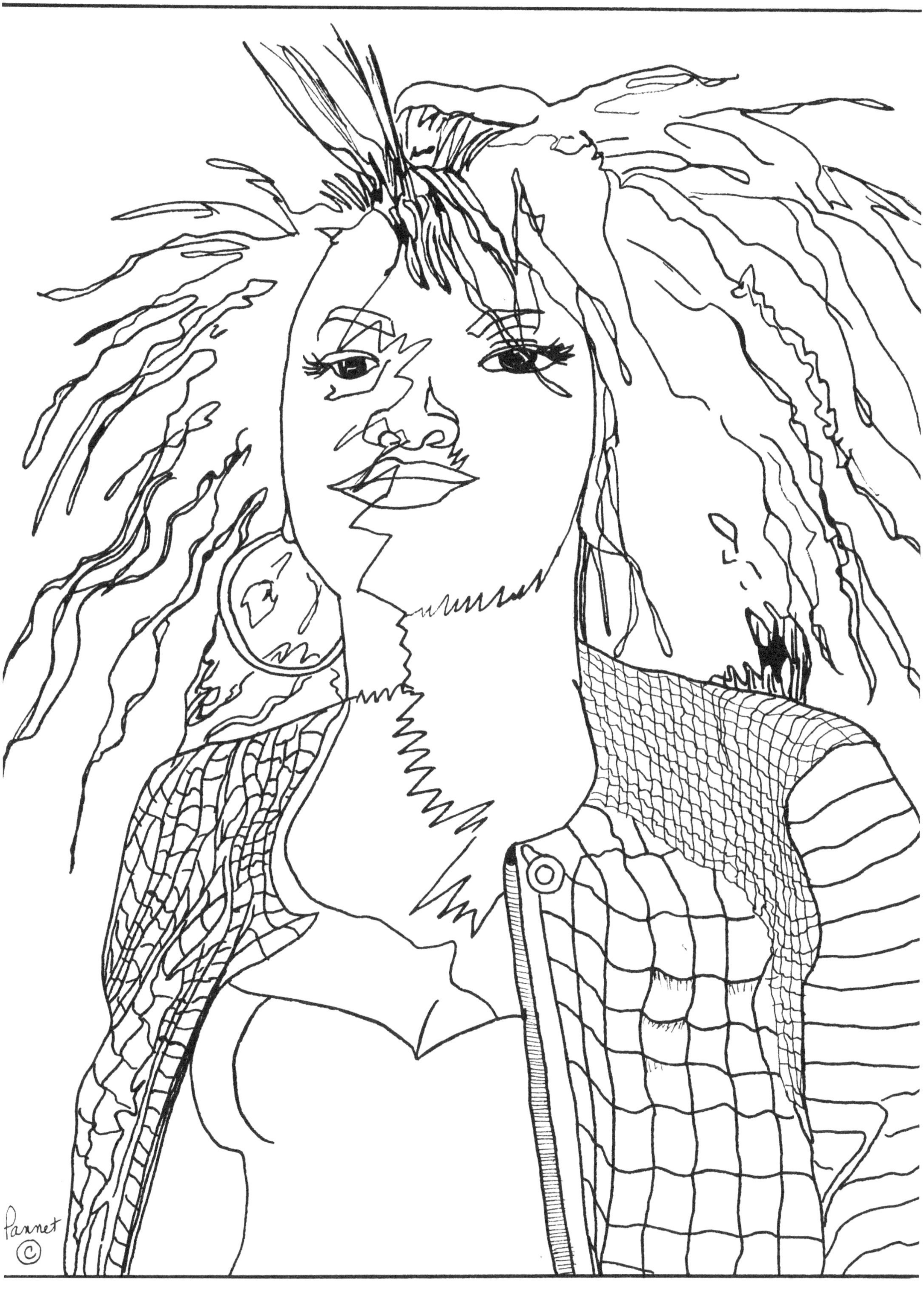
Pannet ©

Notes

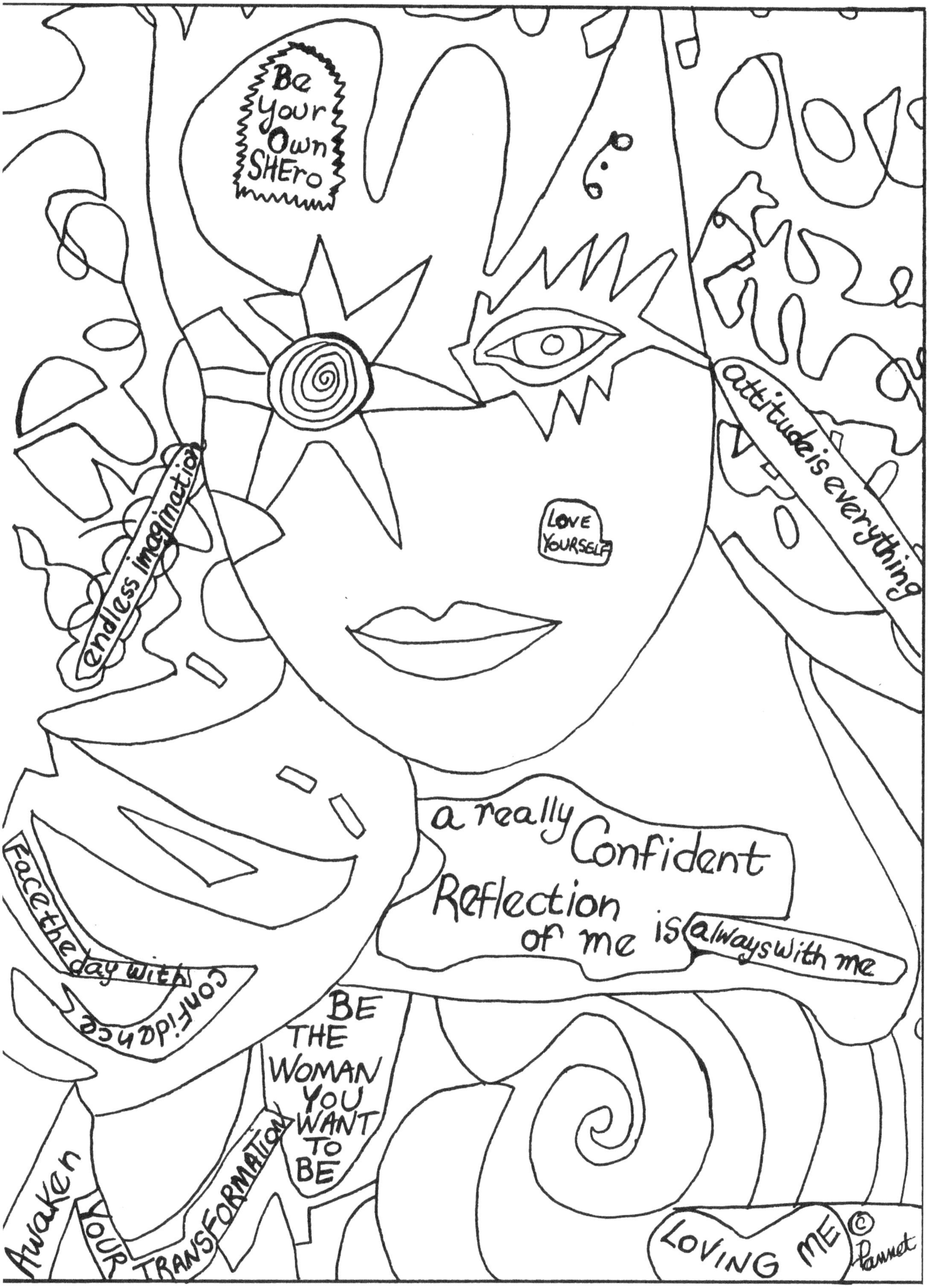
Be your Own SHEro
endless imagination
attitude is everything
LOVE YOURSELF
a really Confident Reflection of me is always with me
Face the day with confidence
BE THE WOMAN YOU WANT TO BE
Awaken YOUR TRANSFORMATION
LOVING ME
© Pannet

Notes

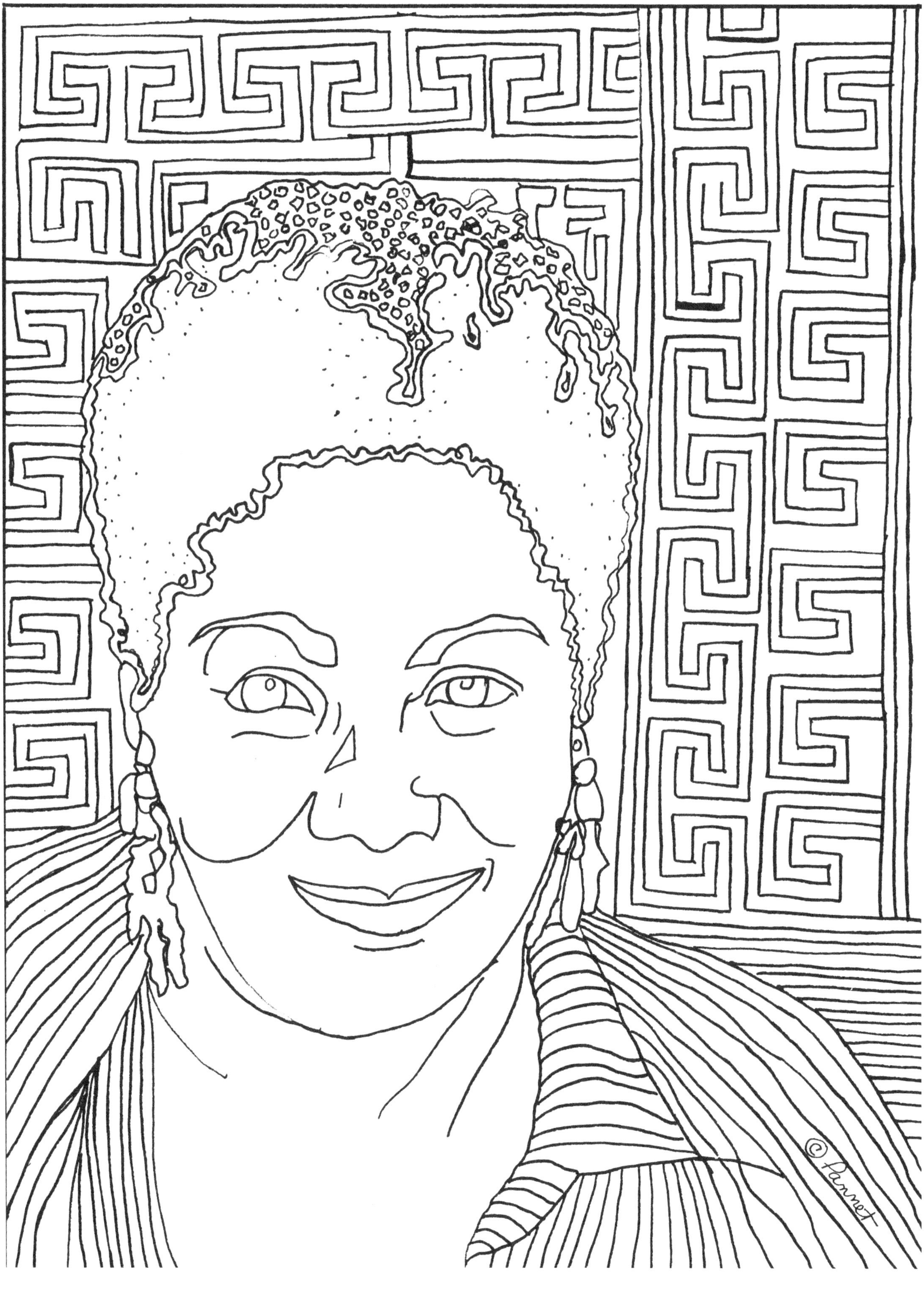
© Pannet

Notes

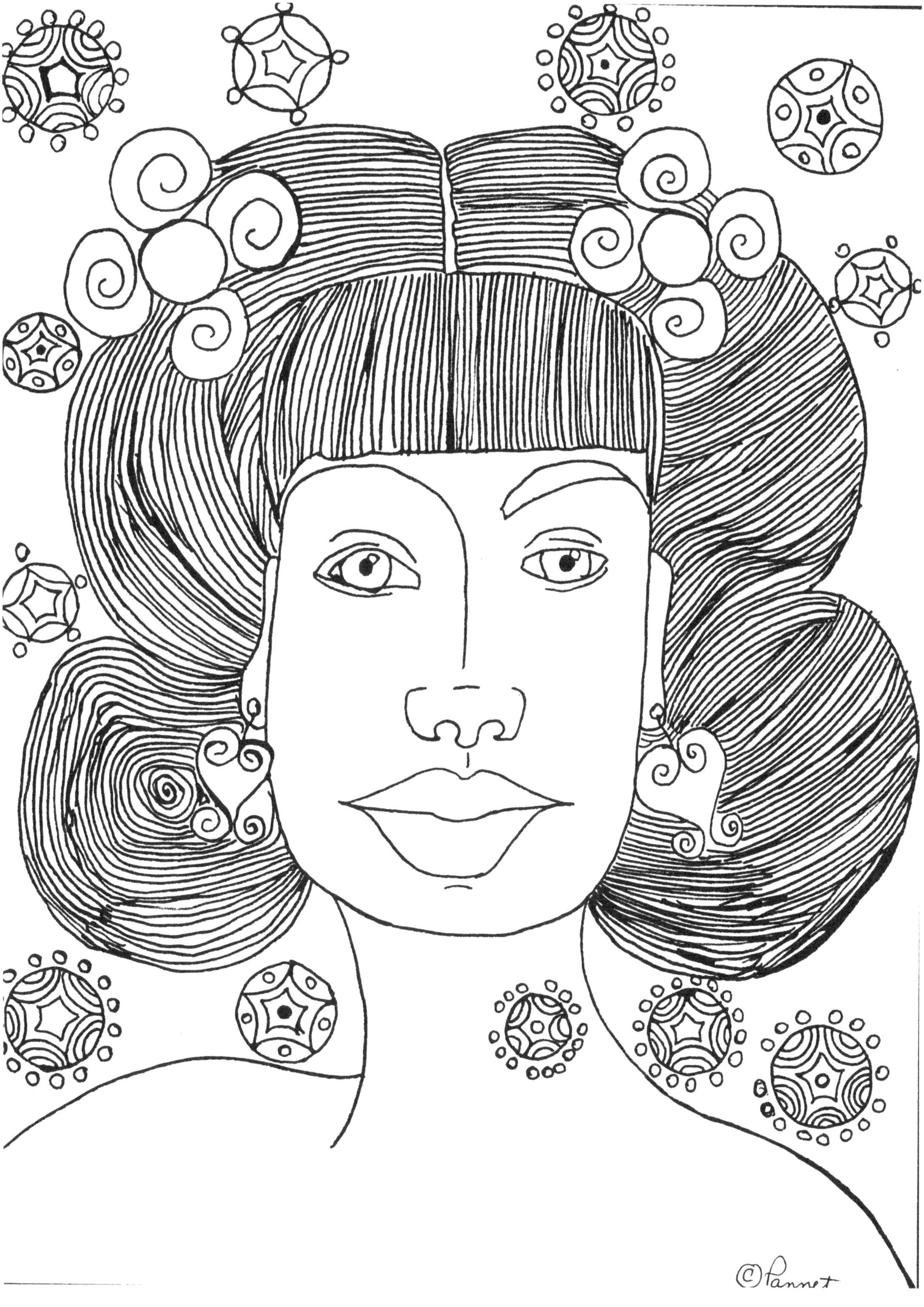
©Pannet

Notes

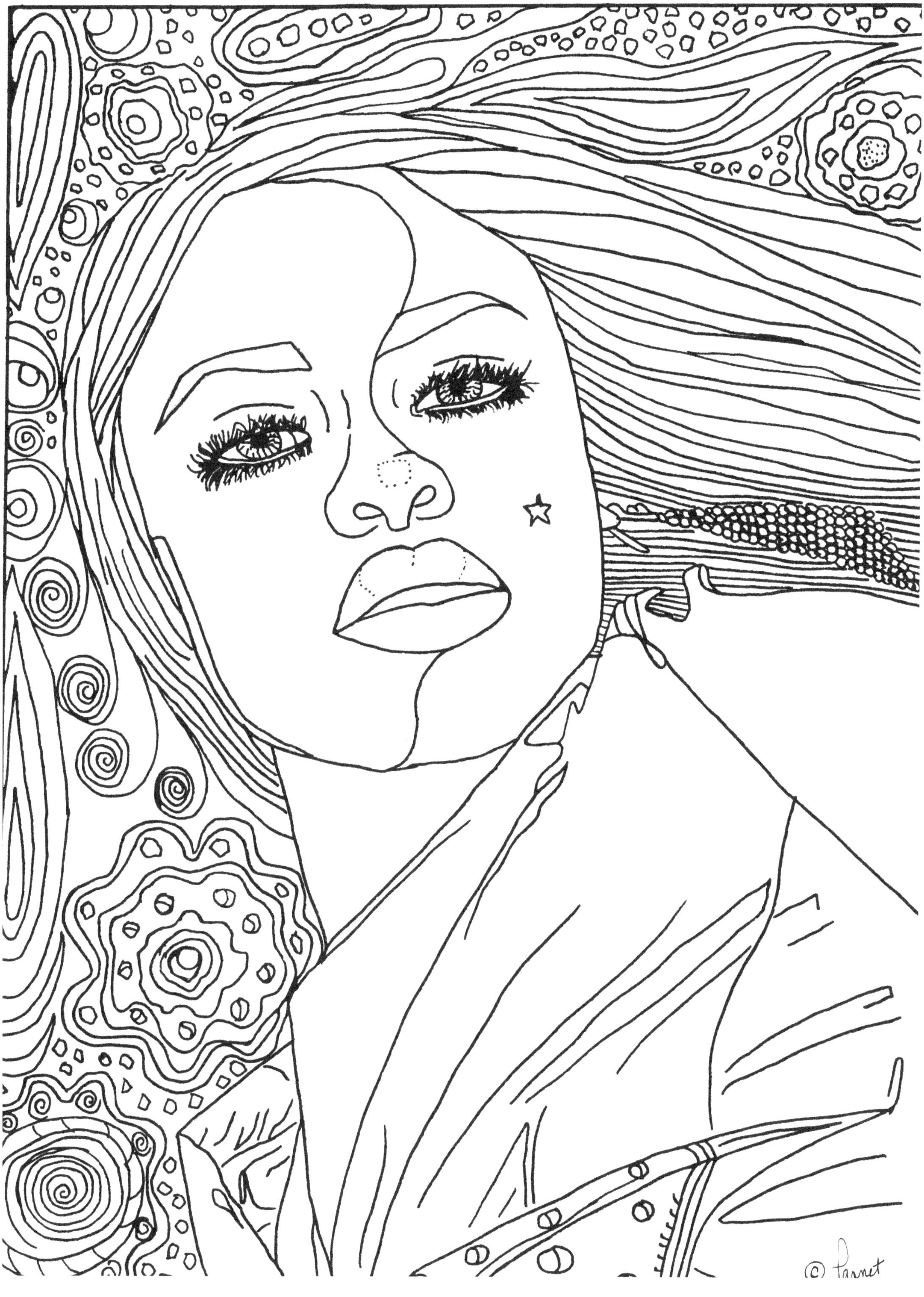
© Parnet

Notes

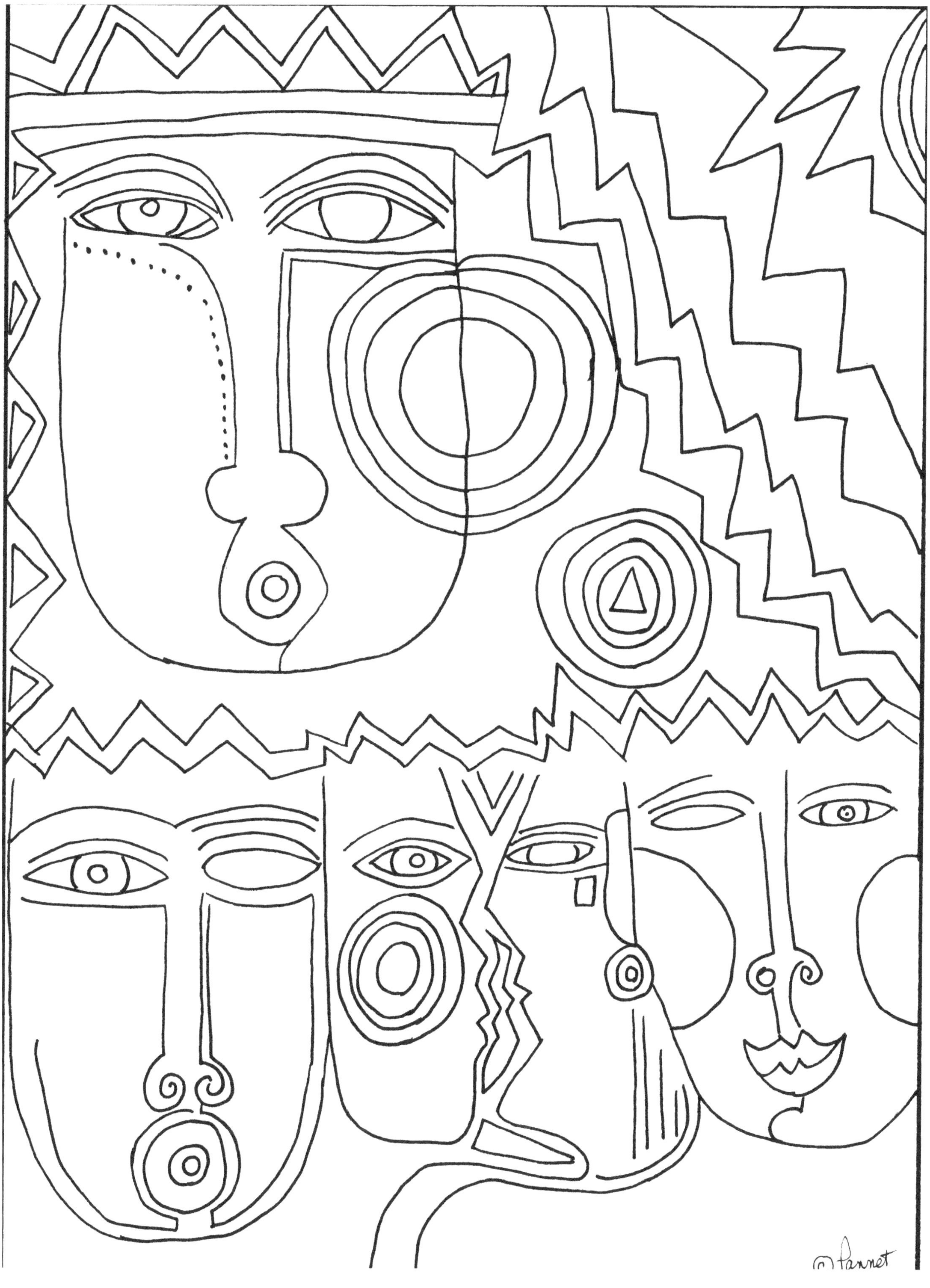
© Pannet

Notes

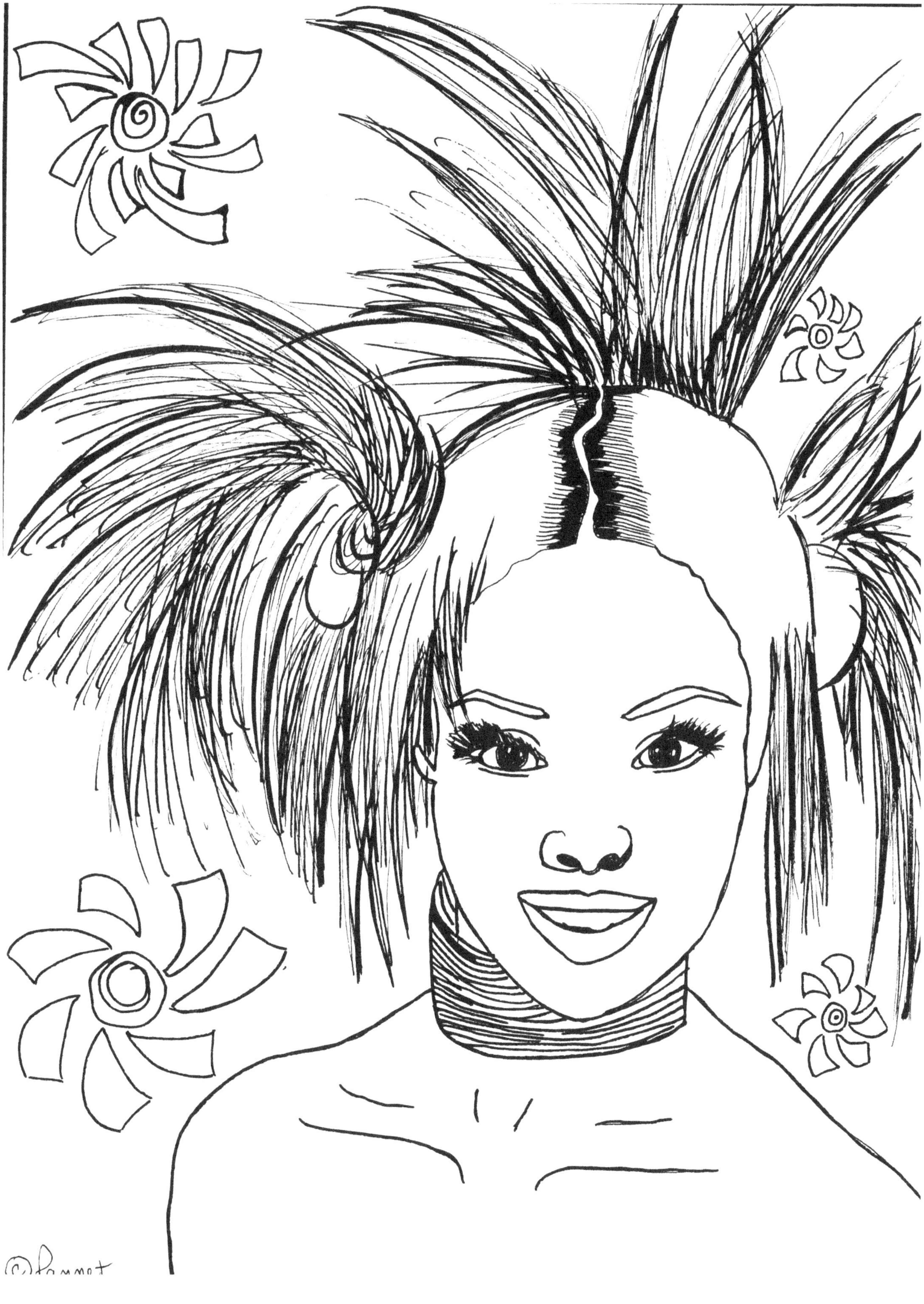

Notes

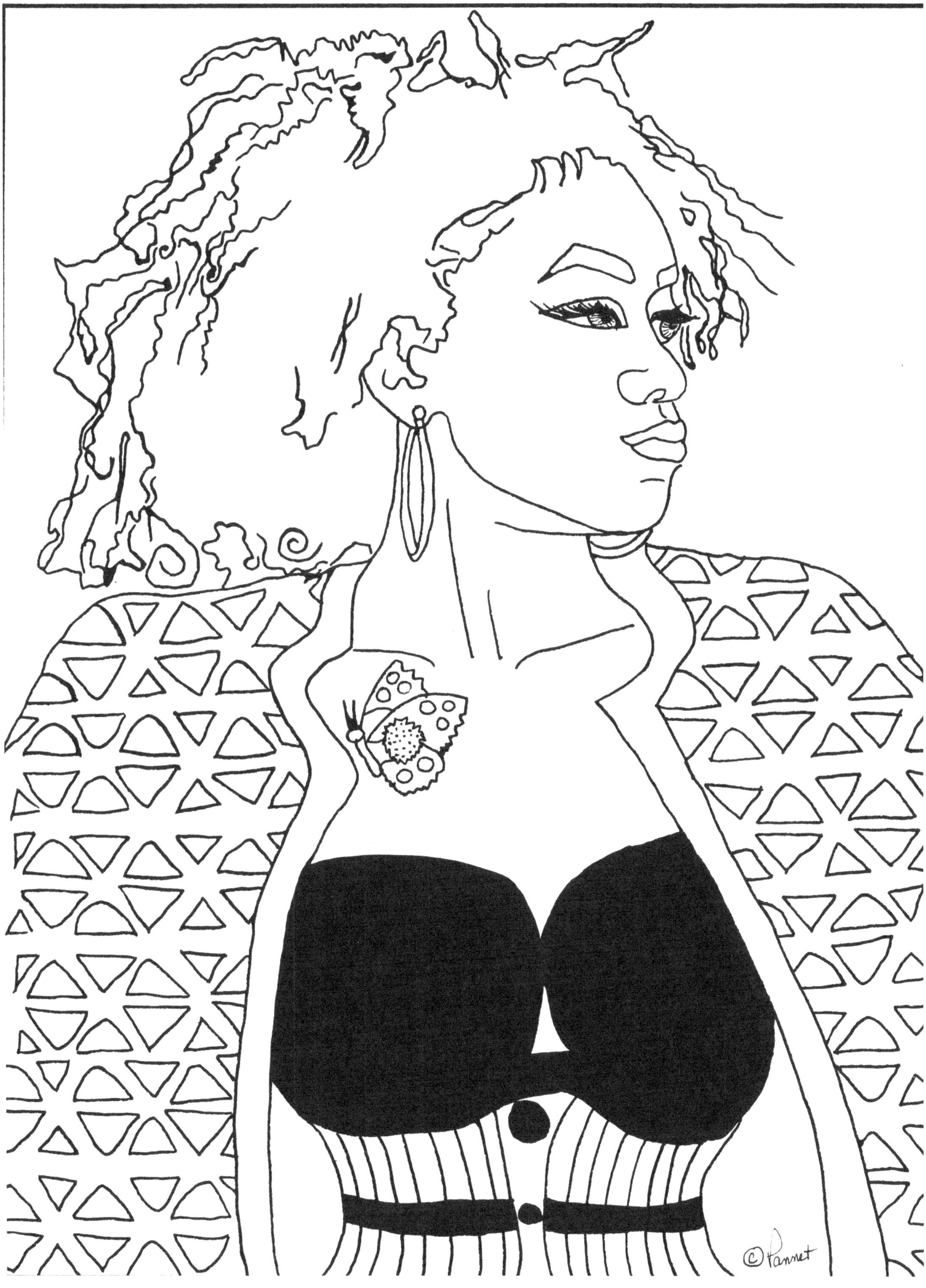
©Pannet

Notes

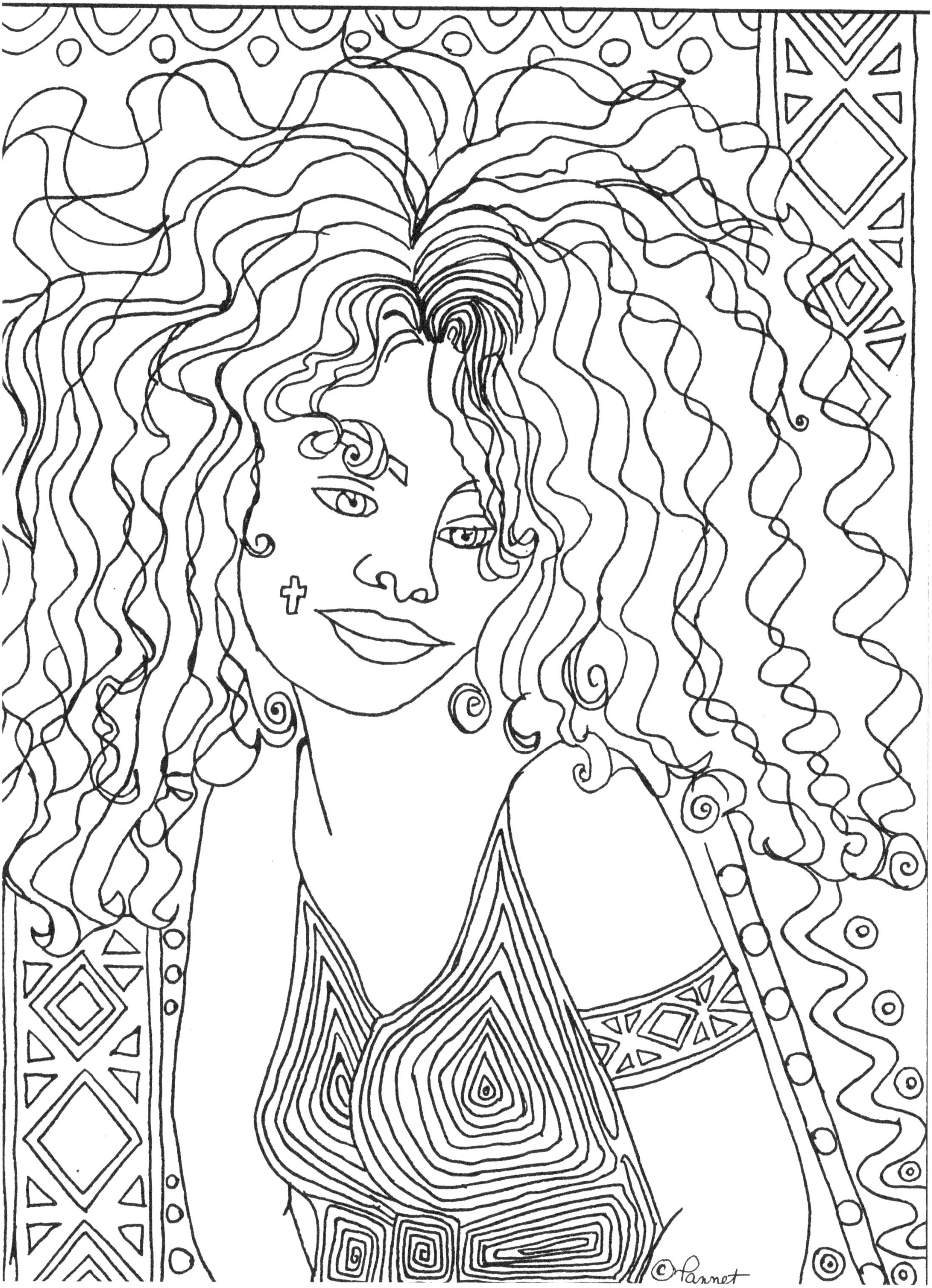
©Pannet

Notes

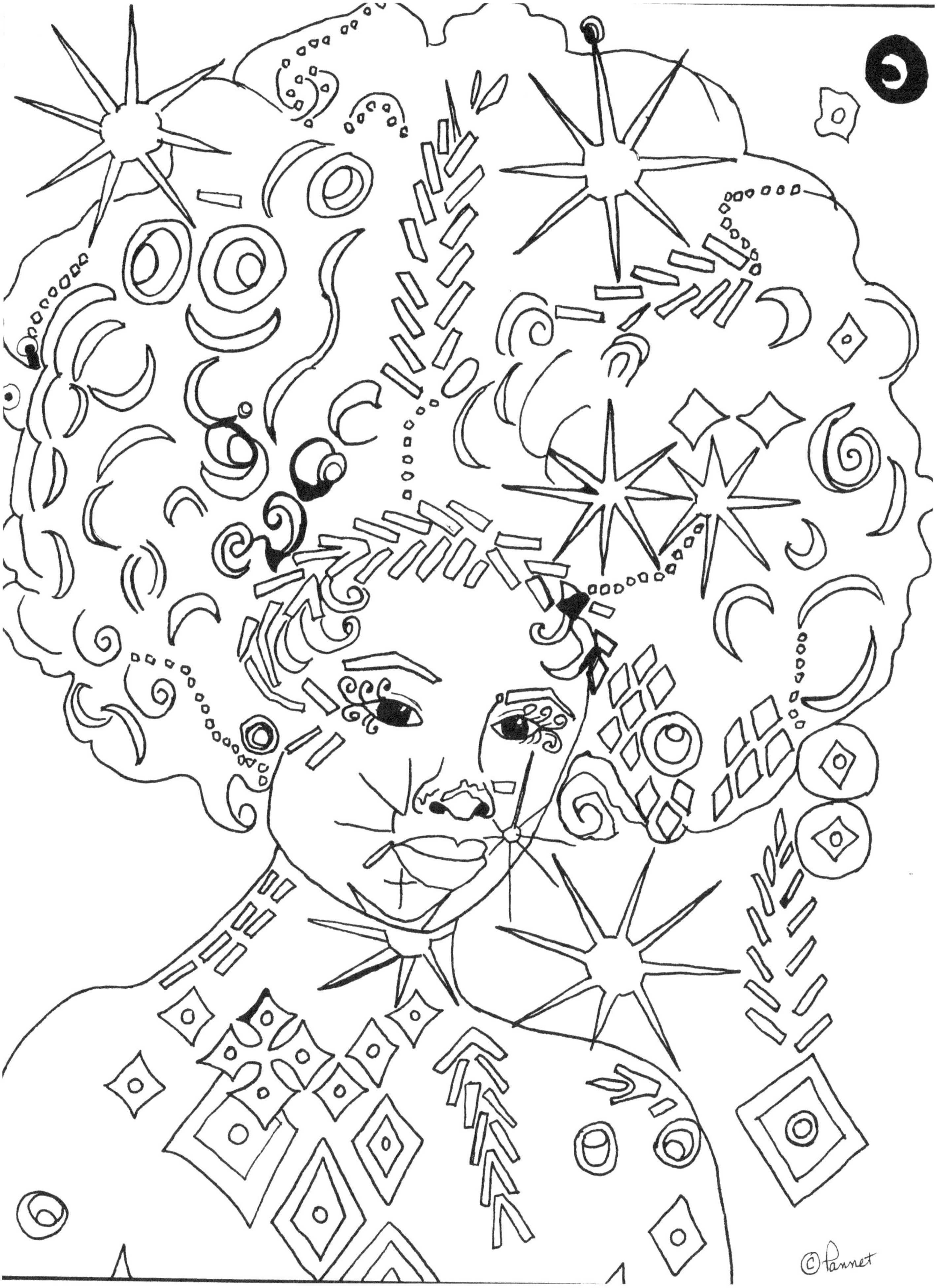
©Pannet

Notes

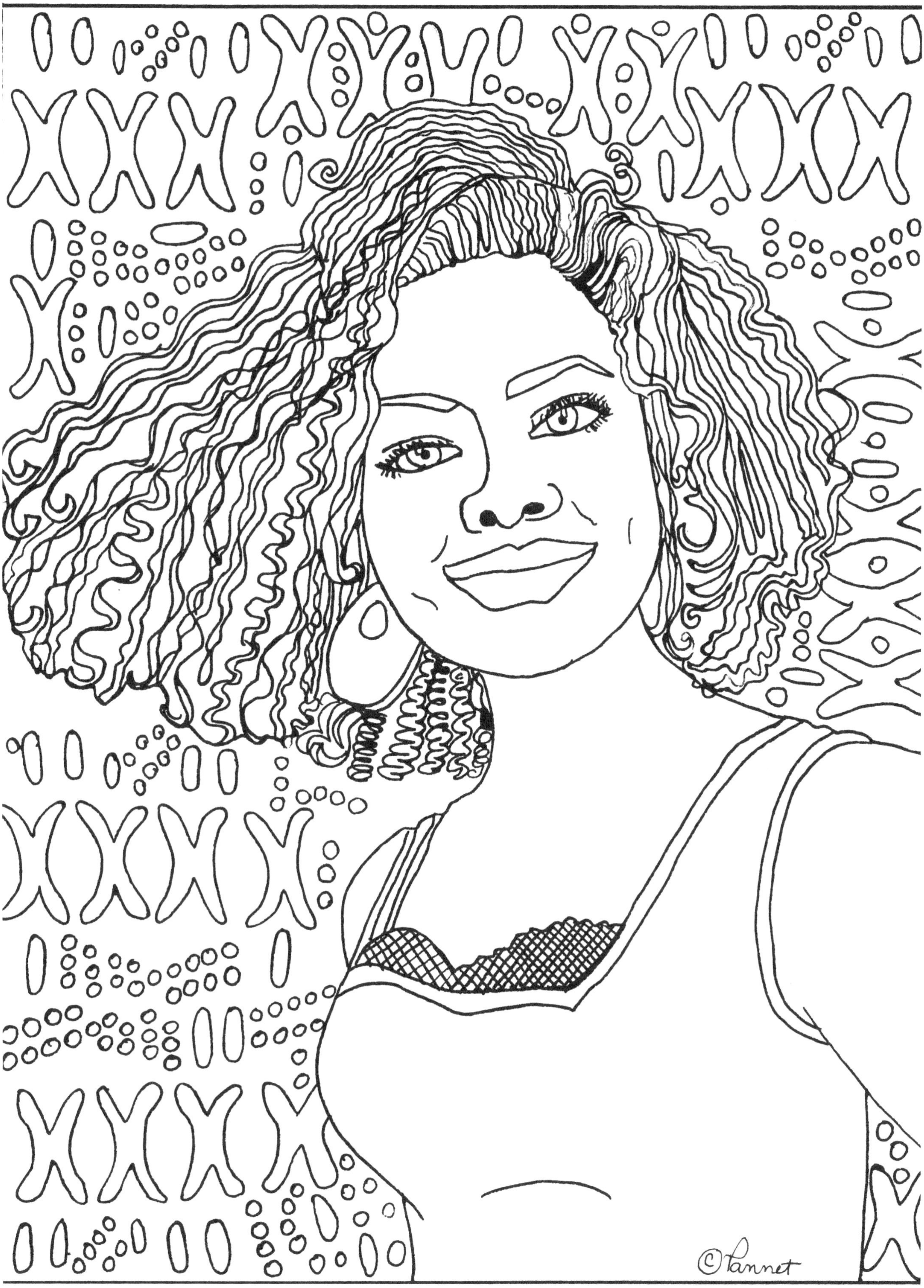
©Pannet

Notes

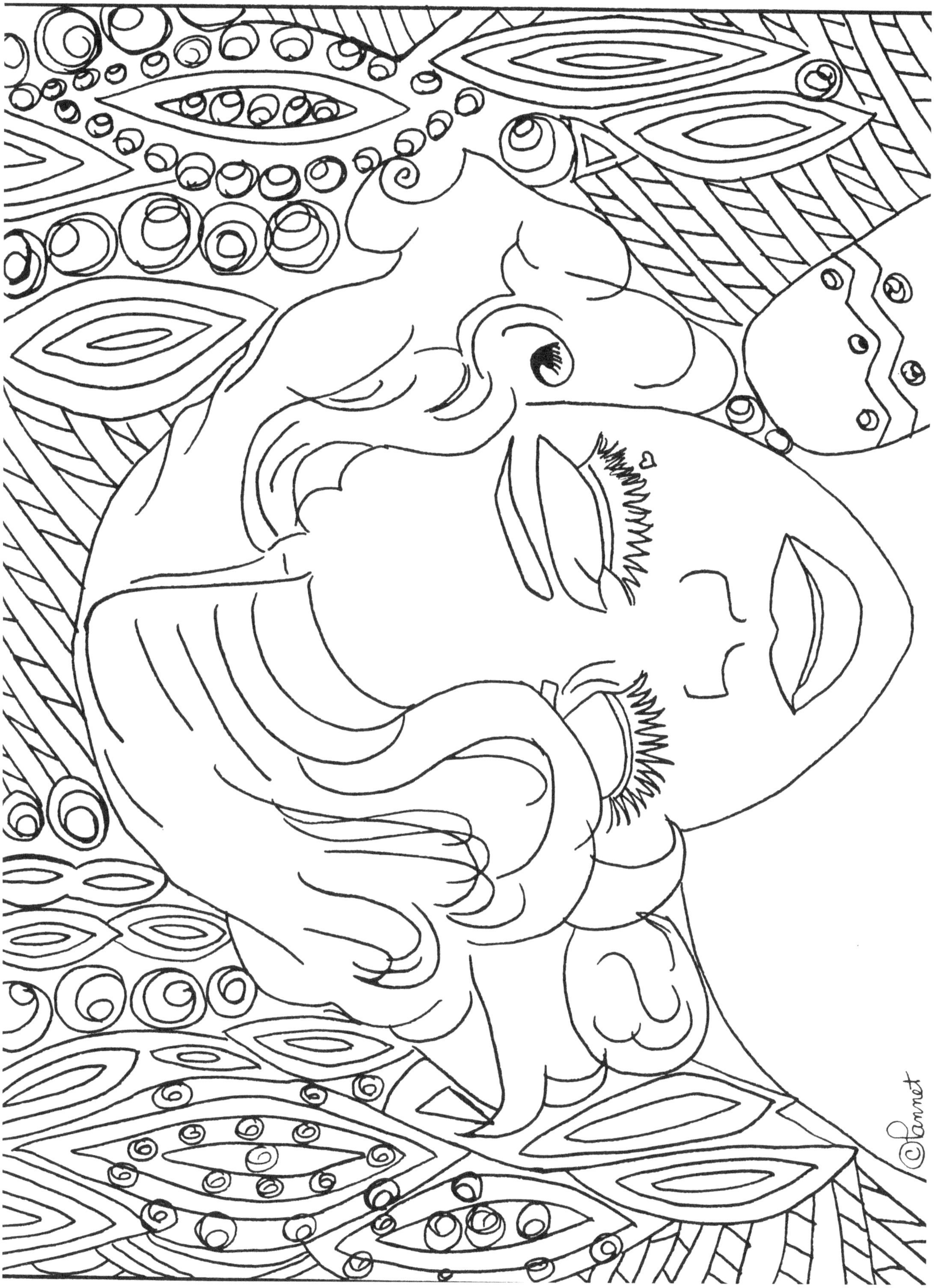

Notes

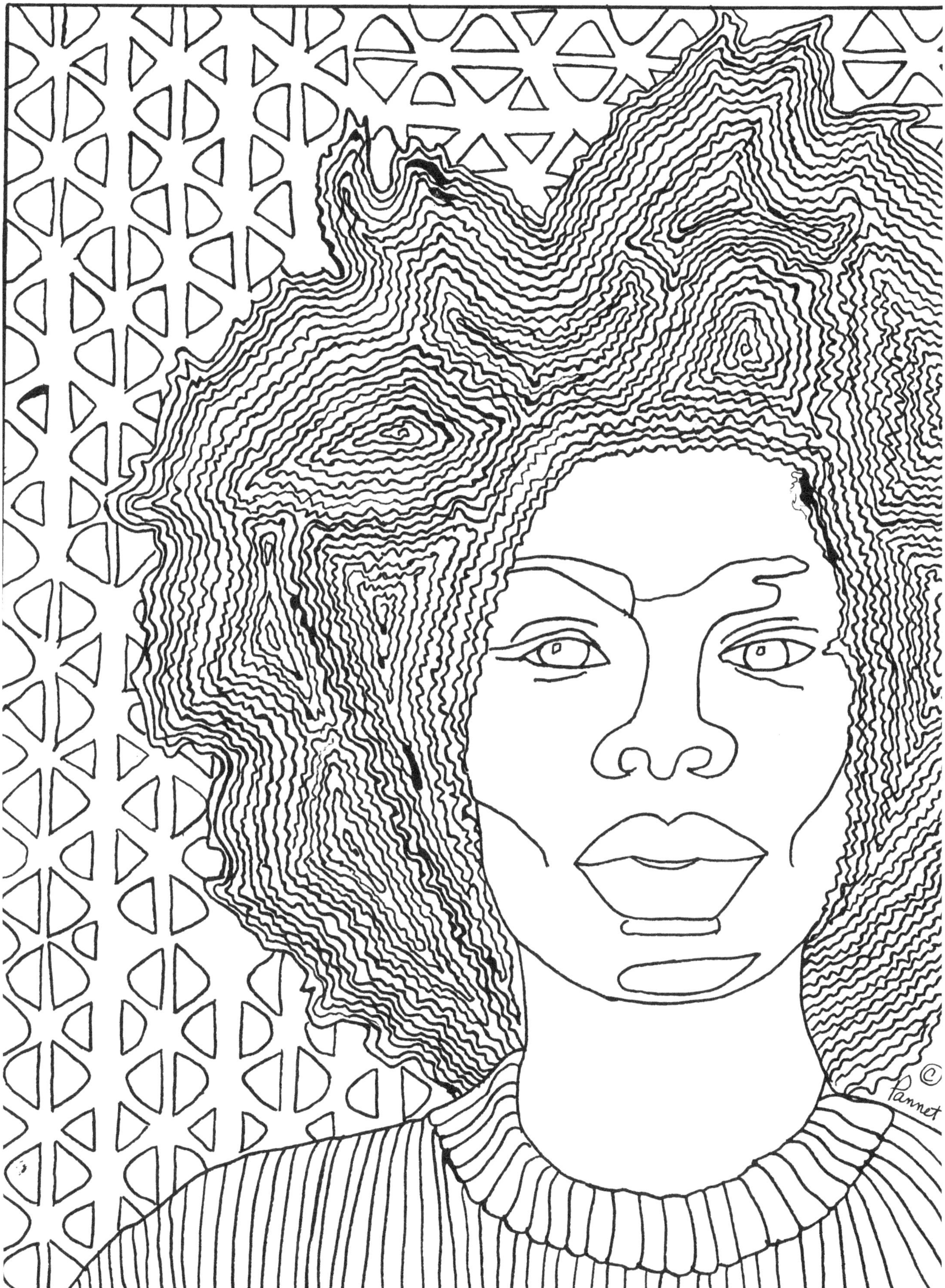
© Pannet

Notes

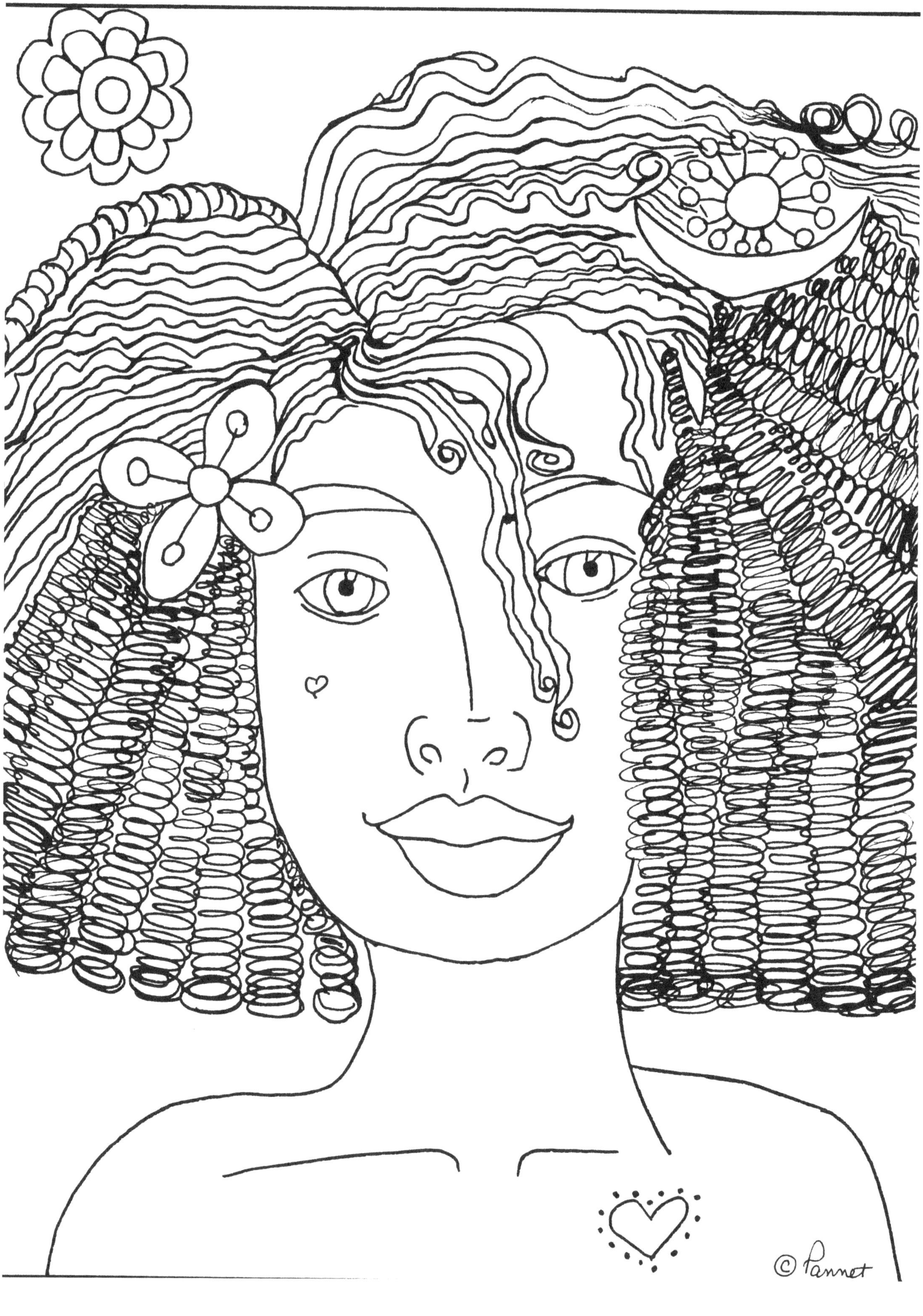
© Pannet

Notes

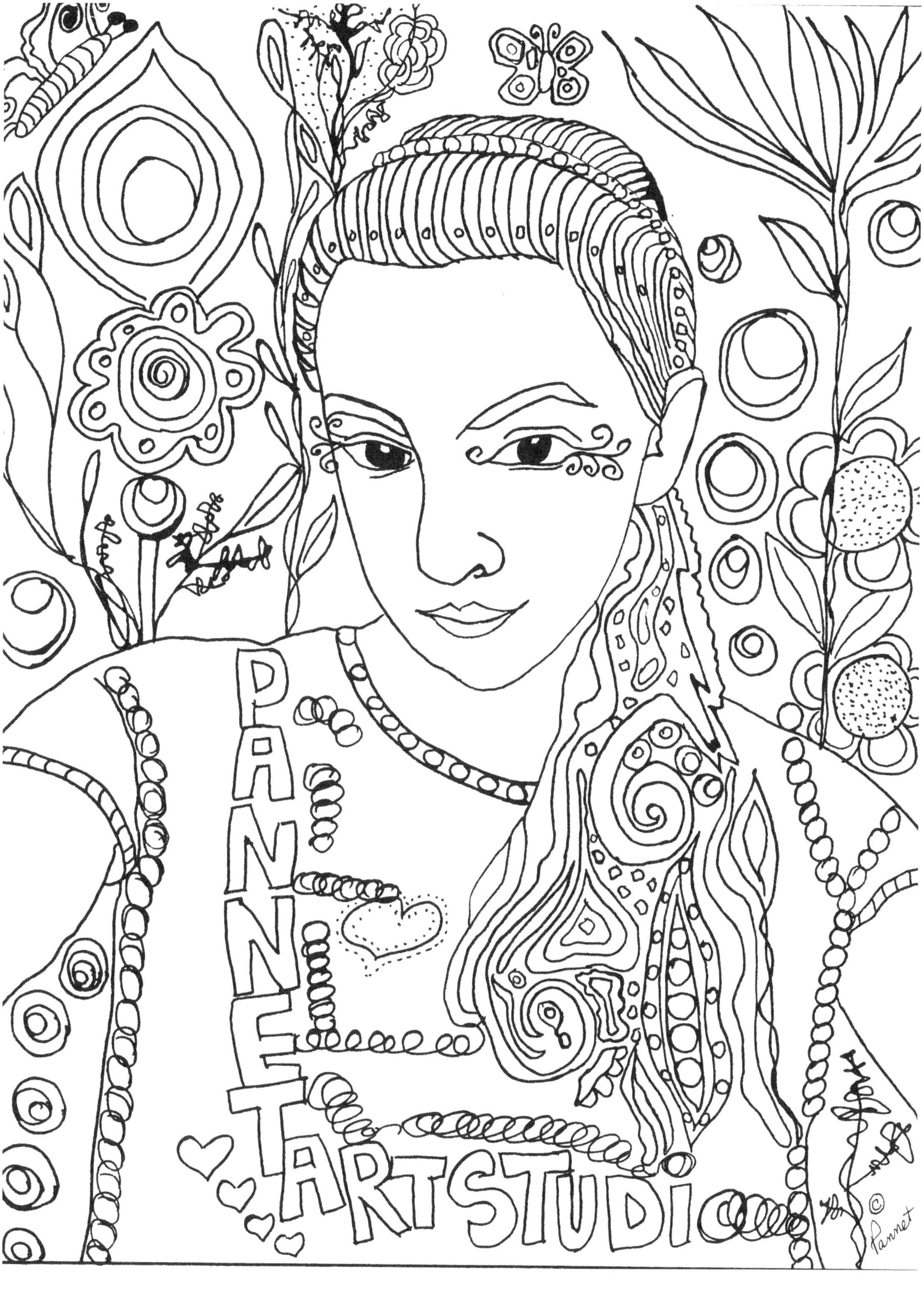
PANNET
ART STUDIO
© Pannet

Notes

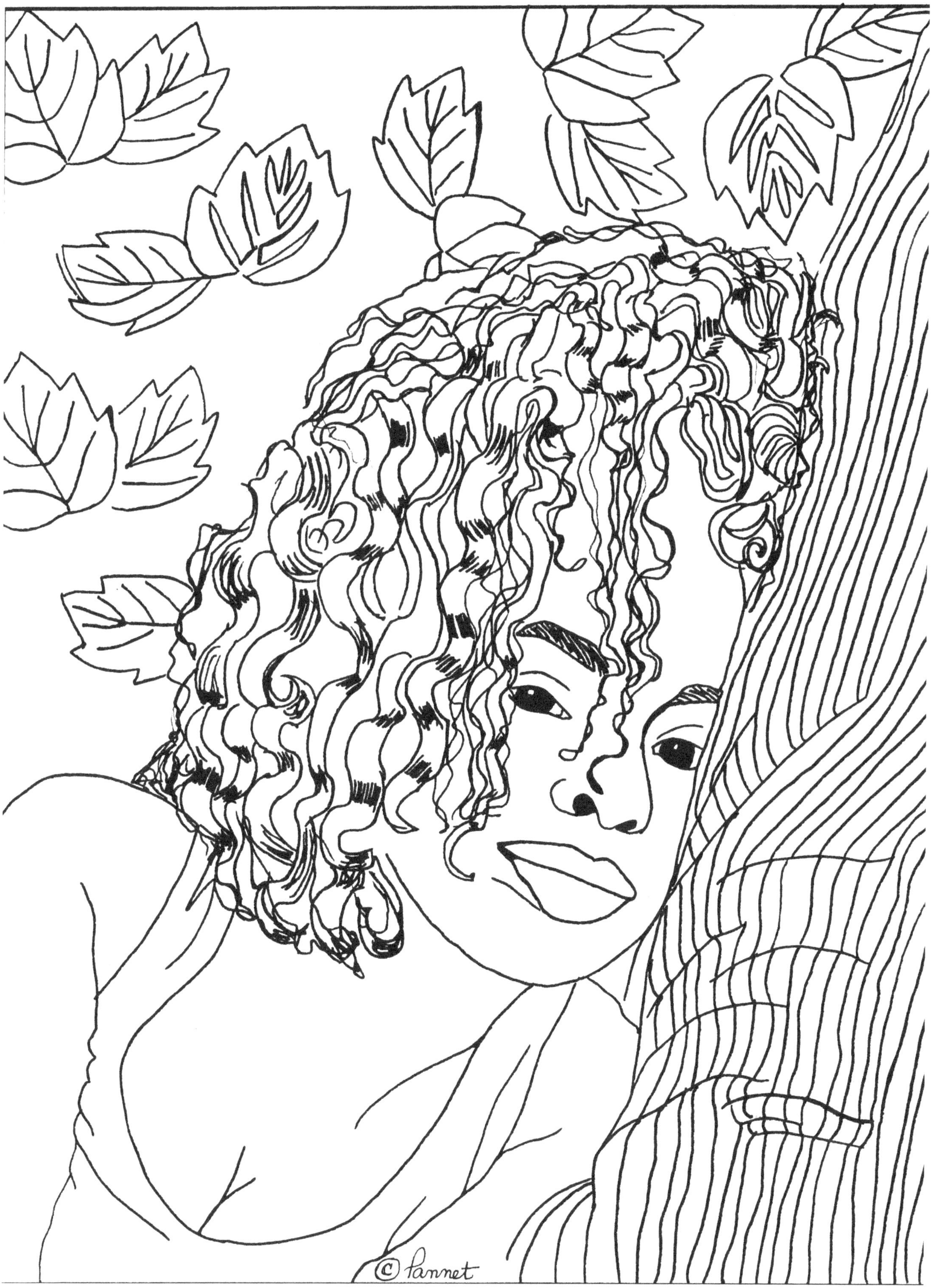
© Pannet

Notes

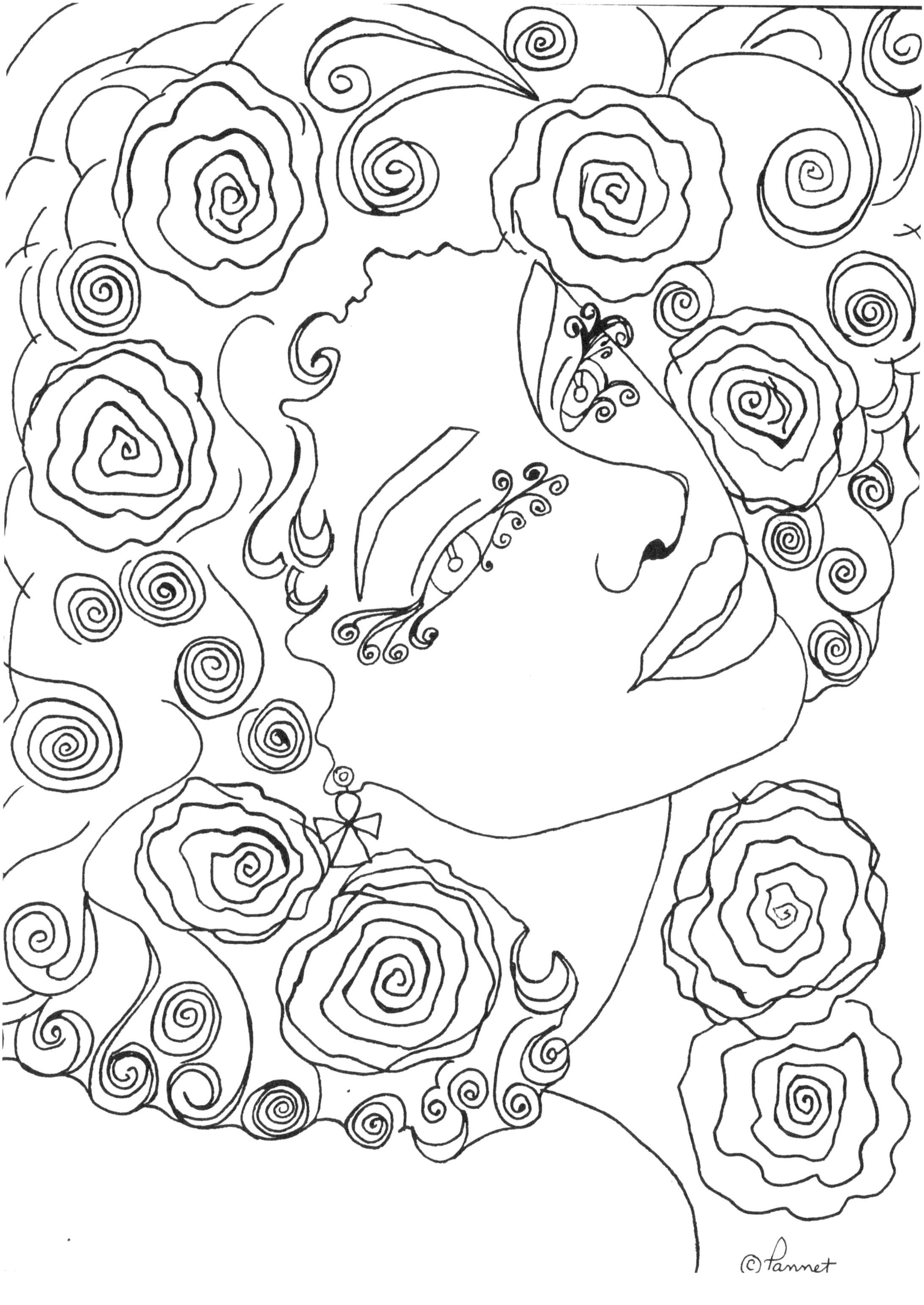
©Pannet

Notes

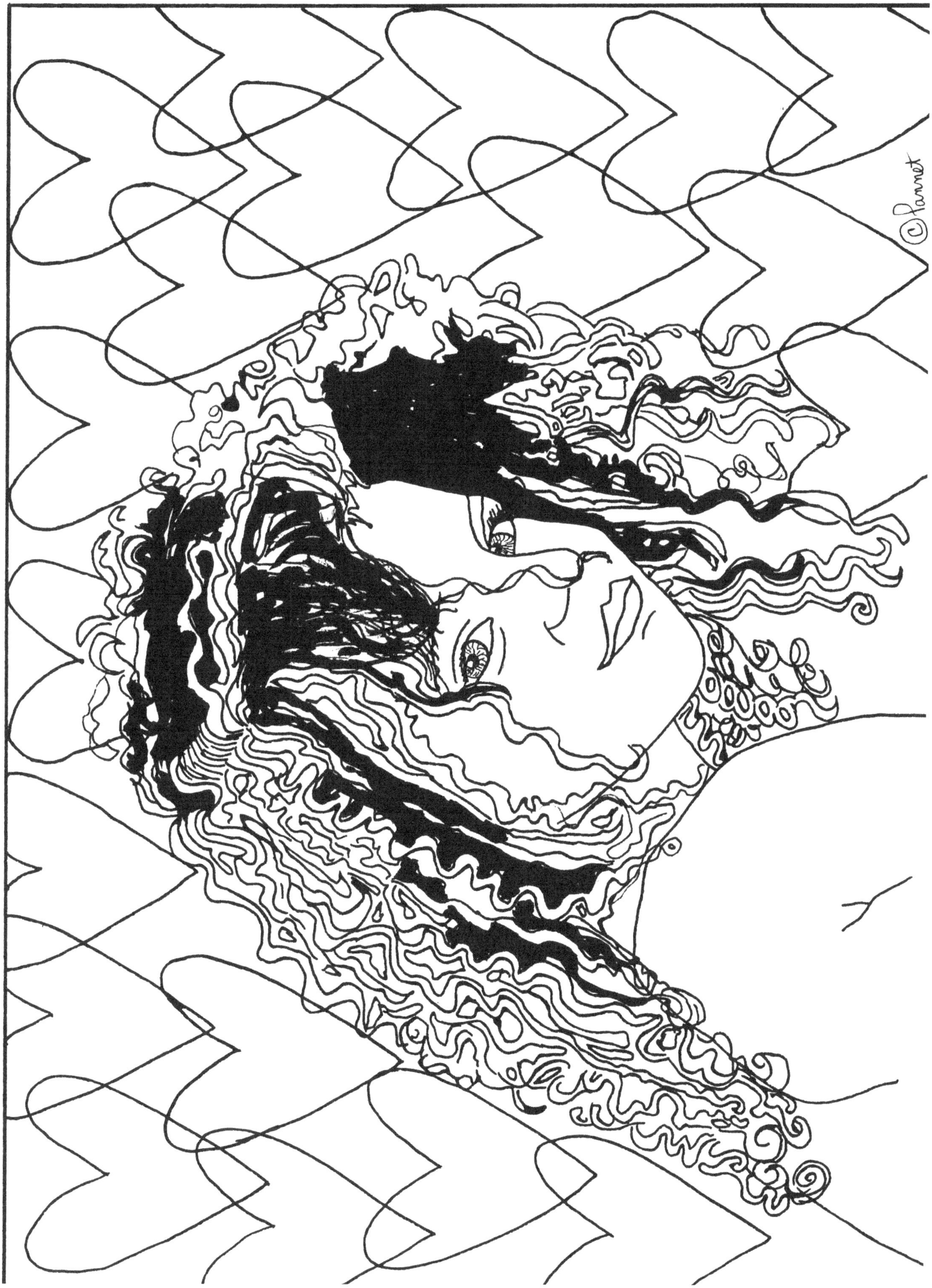
©Pannet

Notes

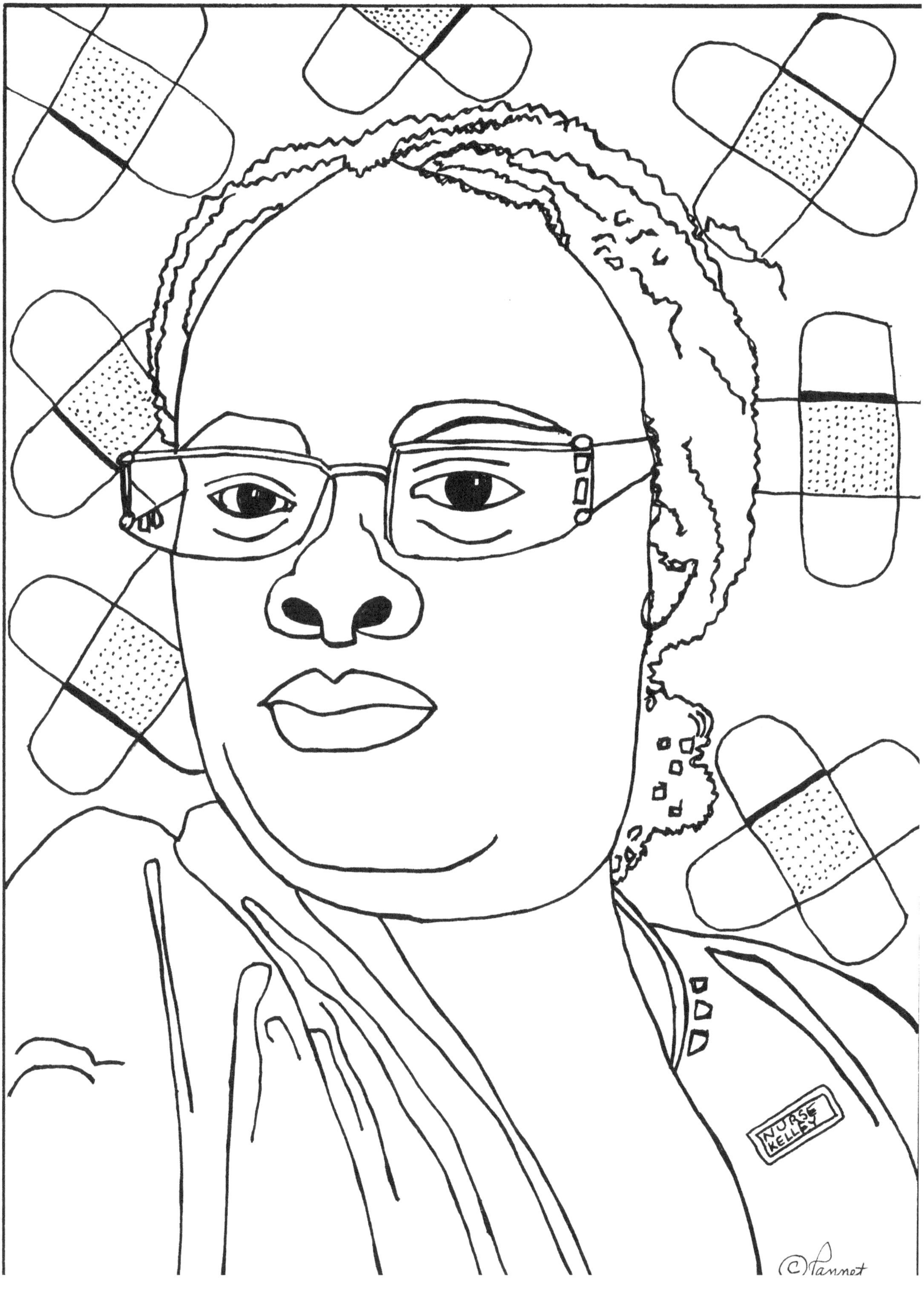
NURSE KELLEY
©Pannet

Notes

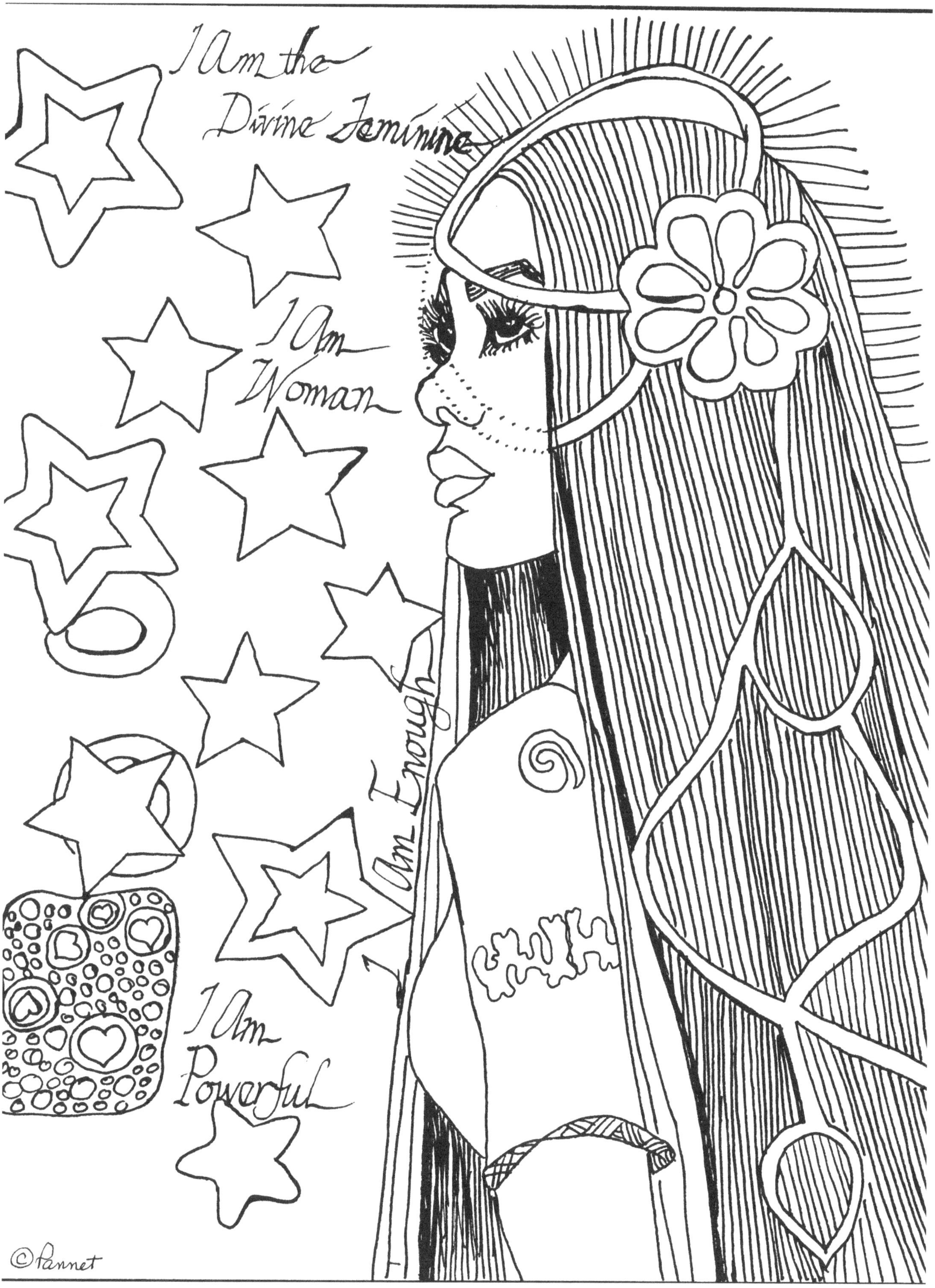
I Am the
Divine Feminine
I Am
Woman
I Am Enough
I Am
Powerful
©Pannet

www.ingramcontent.com/pod-product-compliance
Lightning Source LLC
Chambersburg PA
CBHW080702190526
45169CB00006B/2205
9781537320687